PENGUIN BOOKS

Italian

Italian

Rachael Lane

Contents

Introduction

Italians eat as they live, passionately and with gusto. They take great pleasure in their food and in the company they share it with. Friends and family gather to feast together, share stories and debate who has the best gnocchi recipe! The generosity of the Italian table is evident in meals often three or more courses and stretching on for hours.

Traditional meals begin with a selection of starters (*antipasto*), followed by a small helping of pasta, risotto or a fresh seasonal soup. Fish, meat or poultry, braised and roasted, are served next. A side dish of vegetables or salad, known as the *contorno*, always accompanies the main meal. And finally, the *dolce* or dessert.

This book covers a broad range of traditional-style Italian fare. Gathered from regions across the country, a wide selection of produce, flavors and cooking techniques are used. The recipes are designed to create a satisfying meal on their own or can form part of an Italian feast, to share with family and friends.

Italian Basics

Italian flavors are simple, with the emphasis on local ingredients. Vegetables are homegrown or sourced fresh from marketplaces and produce is used seasonally when flavors are at their best.

The Ingredients

A great deal of care is taken to use quality products. Bread is baked daily. Meats are cured and made into salami, bresaola, pancetta, prosciutto, parma and coppa. Olives are preserved, marinated, stuffed or pressed into oil. Vine-ripened tomatoes are sun-dried or cooked down to make rich pasta sauces and soups. Anchovies are dried and preserved in salt and oil. Ricotta and buffalo mozzarella are made fresh daily. And cheeses like Parmesan, pecorino and fontina are found in many dishes. Pasta—fresh, dried and filled—is ever-present in Italian households. Decadent sweets and pastries are flavored with nuts, liqueurs, chocolate and citrus. And of course at the end of every meal a digestive such as grappa or limoncello is served, followed by an espresso.

Regional Influences

The food of Italy changes from region to region, each having its own speciality. In the North, the terrain is mountainous and the climate is cooler. Short-grain rice such as arborio is grown here, packaged and sold as risotto. However, the land is better suited to grazing than to growing crops. Veal, beef and pork are reared, and used to produce spicy sausages, salami and other cured meats. Warm nourishing dishes such as slow-cooked and braised meats, thick polenta and hearty broths come from this region.

In the South, the climate is hotter and the food tends to be lighter. Tomatoes, olives, bell peppers, eggplants, artichokes, garlic, oranges, lemons and nuts are grown here. Fish and seafood such as tuna, swordfish, sea bream, sea bass, squid, oysters, mussels and clams are in abundant supply and can be found on most menus. Dried fruits and fresh herbs such as rosemary, basil, parsley, mint, fennel and oregano are used to flavor dishes.

The Italian Kitchen

There are a few essential items used in the pasta recipes including a large pasta pot, slotted spoon, and fluted dough wheel (though this can easily be replaced with a sharp knife). Other recipes call for 10-inch pizza trays, cannoli tubes, a pastry bag and piping nozzles. All are available from kitchenware stores.

If you plan to make homemade pasta, the most useful piece of equipment is a pasta machine. There are numerous varieties available, most reasonably inexpensive to buy, and they will knead, roll and even cut the dough for you. Always brush out any excess flour after use and store in a clean, dry place. (Never wash your pasta machine, it will cause it to rust.)

Starters

A traditional Italian meal begins with the antipasto—a selection of hot and cold appetizers shared amongst guests. Most of the starters that follow can be offered as antipasti.

If preparing one or two dishes only, team them with some cured meats, cheese and crostini.

< STUFFED MUSSELS (PAGE 8)

Stuffed Mussels

SERVES 4–6

2 pounds 3 ounces black
mussels
½ cup dry white wine
1 tablespoon olive oil
½ small onion, finely diced
1 garlic clove, finely chopped
2 anchovy fillets, finely
chopped
2 tablespoons finely chopped
fresh parsley

2 tablespoons finely chopped
fresh oregano
1 teaspoon finely grated lemon
zest
1 cup breadcrumbs, made
from day-old country-style
bread
salt and freshly ground black
pepper
extra-virgin olive oil, to serve

Preheat the oven to 400°F.

Scrub the mussels, discarding any shells that remain open. Remove the beards
and rinse clean.

Place the mussels and wine in a large saucepan over high heat. Cover and
cook for 4–5 minutes, until opened. (Discard any unopened mussels.) Arrange
mussels, in the half shell, in a single layer on a baking sheet.

Heat the olive oil in a fry pan over low–medium heat. Add the onion and garlic and sauté until softened. Add the anchovies and sauté an additional minute, until dissolved. Stir in the parsley, oregano, lemon zest and breadcrumbs. Season with salt and pepper.

Sprinkle the crumb mixture over the mussels to cover. Drizzle with extra-virgin olive oil and bake in the oven for 10 minutes, until golden-brown.

Fried Whitebait

SERVES 4–6

piece of bread, to test olive oil
olive oil, for deep-frying
¾ cup all-purpose flour
salt and freshly ground black
    pepper
1 pound 2 ounce whitebait
1 lemon, cut into wedges

Half-fill a heavy-based saucepan with olive oil. Heat the olive oil to 350°F or until a piece of bread browns in 15 seconds when tested.

Place the flour in a small bowl and season with salt and pepper. Dry the whitebait using paper towel and toss it in the flour, shaking off any excess. Fry the whitebait in batches for 4–5 minutes, turning occasionally until crisp and golden-brown. Remove using a slotted spoon and drain on paper towels. Season with salt.

Serve with lemon wedges.

೧ Whitebait is young fish; especially herring.

Zucchini Frittata

2 tablespoons olive oil
1 small onion, finely sliced
2 cloves garlic, finely chopped
3 small zucchini, trimmed and
   thinly sliced
8 large eggs, lightly beaten

4 ounces ricotta, crumbled
½ cup shaved salted ricotta
3 tablespoons finely chopped
   mint
salt and freshly ground black
   pepper

Preheat broiler to medium–high.

Heat the olive oil in a 9-inch ovenproof fry pan over low–medium heat. Add the onion and garlic and sauté until softened. Add the zucchini and sauté for 4–6 minutes, until golden-brown.

Spread the zucchini evenly over the bottom of the pan and pour in the egg mixture. Scatter the ricotta, salted ricotta and mint over the top. Season with salt and pepper and cook for 5–8 minutes over low–medium heat, until almost set. Place pan under the broiler and cook an additional 2 minutes, until the cheese has melted and frittata is completely set.

Slice into portions. Serve warm or at room temperature.

Tomato, Basil & Mozzarella Bruschetta

SERVES 4

2 medium vine-ripened
  tomatoes, diced
½ cup fresh basil leaves, torn
1 ball buffalo mozzarella, torn
4 tablespoons extra-virgin
  olive oil

salt and freshly ground black
  pepper
4 thin slices country-style
  bread
1 clove garlic, halved

Preheat grill or broiler to medium–high.

Place the tomato, basil and mozzarella in a medium bowl. Add 1 tablespoon of the olive oil and season with salt and pepper, and toss to combine.

Grill or broil the bread until golden-brown. Rub the garlic over the bread on one side and drizzle with the remaining olive oil. Top the bread with the tomato mixture and serve immediately.

Carpaccio

SERVES 4

10 ounce beef fillet
¼ cup thinly shaved Parmesan
    cheese, to serve
freshly ground black pepper

MAYONNAISE
1 large egg yolk
1 tablespoon red-wine vinegar
1 teaspoon Dijon mustard
½ clove garlic, crushed
½ cup olive oil
salt and freshly ground black
    pepper

Place four serving plates in the refrigerator to chill until serving.

Trim the beef removing any fat or tough fibers. Tightly wrap the beef in several layers of food wrap, creating a round shape and covering the meat entirely. Place in the freezer for 45–60 minutes, until firm, but not frozen.

To make the mayonnaise, combine the egg yolk, vinegar, mustard and garlic together in a medium-sized bowl. Gradually add the olive oil in a thin stream, whisking continuously until thick and creamy. Season with salt and pepper.

Unwrap the beef and cut wafer-thin slices using a very sharp knife. Arrange the slices on the chilled plates, with slices overlapping slightly. Drizzle with mayonnaise, scatter with Parmesan cheese and season with pepper.

Sardines with Raisins & Pine Nuts

SERVES 4

1¾ pounds sardines, scaled,
cleaned and boned
2 tablespoons extra-virgin
olive oil

FILLING
²/₃ cup coarsely chopped
breadcrumbs, made from
day-old country-style bread
2 tablespoons extra-virgin
olive oil
2 tablespoons raisins

2 tablespoons pine nuts, lightly
toasted
2 tablespoons finely grated
Parmesan cheese
1 tablespoon finely chopped
fresh flat-leaf parsley leaves
1 tablespoon finely chopped
fresh rosemary
1 tablespoon lemon juice
1 clove garlic, finely chopped
salt and freshly ground black
pepper

Preheat the oven to 325°F.

To make filling, place the breadcrumbs on a baking sheet and drizzle with the olive oil. Bake in the oven for 10–15 minutes, until golden-brown. Finely chop and set aside.

Increase the oven temperature to 400°F. Lightly oil a baking dish.

Combine the breadcrumbs, raisins, pine nuts, Parmesan cheese, parsley, rosemary, lemon juice and garlic in a small bowl. Season with salt and pepper.

Spoon the filling into the sardine cavities and arrange the sardines on the baking dish in a single layer. Drizzle with the olive oil and bake in the oven for 10–15 minutes, until golden-brown.

Serve warm or at room temperature.

Baked Eggplant & Ricotta Rolls

SERVES 4

2 medium long eggplants
4 tablespoons olive oil
14 ounces fresh firm ricotta
1 cup grated Pecorino cheese
2 tablespoons finely chopped
  fresh basil
2 tablespoons finely chopped
  fresh oregano
2 tablespoons finely chopped
  fresh thyme
¼ cup basil pesto

TOMATO SAUCE
2 tablespoons extra-virgin
  olive oil
1 small onion, diced
1 clove garlic, finely chopped
1 (14½-ounce) can crushed
  tomatoes
1 tablespoon tomato paste
½ teaspoon sugar
salt and freshly ground black
  pepper

Preheat the oven to 400°F.

To make the sauce, heat the olive oil in a heavy-based saucepan over low–medium heat. Add the onion and garlic and sauté until softened. Add the tomatoes, tomato paste and sugar and bring to a boil. Decrease the heat to low and gently simmer for 20 minutes. Remove from the heat and let cool slightly. Pour into a food processor or blender and blend until puréed. Season with salt and pepper. >

Cut the eggplants lengthwise into thin slices.

Heat half of the olive oil in a large, non-stick fry pan over medium heat. Grill half of the eggplant slices for 2 minutes on each side, until golden-brown. Repeat with the remaining olive oil and eggplant.

Combine the ricotta with half of the Pecorino cheese, and the basil, oregano and thyme in a medium bowl. Season with salt and pepper. Spread over the eggplant slices and roll up lengthwise.

Spoon one third of the sauce into a small baking dish. Arrange the eggplant rolls, seam side down, in the dish and cover with the remaining sauce. Scatter spoonfuls of pesto over the top and sprinkle with remaining Pecorino cheese. Cover with aluminum foil and bake in the oven for 20 minutes. Uncover and bake an additional 5–10 minutes, until cheese is golden-brown.

Fried Zucchini Flowers

SERVES 4

12 zucchini flowers with baby
   zucchini attached
$\frac{1}{3}$ cup all-purpose flour
$\frac{3}{4}$ cup water
vegetable oil, for deep-frying
piece of bread, to test vegetable
   oil

FILLING
$1\frac{3}{4}$ ounces ricotta cheese
$1\frac{3}{4}$ ounces soft goat cheese

1 tablespoon grated Parmesan
   cheese
1 tablespoon finely chopped
   fresh basil
1 tablespoon finely chopped
   fresh mint
$\frac{1}{2}$ teaspoon finely grated
   lemon zest
salt and freshly ground black
   pepper

Combine the ricotta, goat cheese, Parmesan cheese, basil, mint and lemon zest in a bowl. Season with salt and pepper. Gently open the zucchini flowers and spoon a heaping teaspoon of the mixture inside. Close to encase the filling.

Combine the flour and water in a bowl, stirring to make a smooth batter.

Half-fill a large, heavy-based saucepan with vegetable oil for deep-frying. Heat the vegetable oil to 350°F or until a piece of bread browns in 15 seconds. Dip the flowers in batter and fry in batches, turning occasionally, for 3-4 minutes, until crisp and golden-brown. Remove using a slotted spoon and drain on paper towels. Season with salt.

Roasted Bell Pepper, Basil & Fontina Arancini

SERVES 6

6 tablespoons butter
1 tablespoon olive oil
1 small onion, finely chopped
2 cloves garlic, finely chopped
1 cup arborio rice
½ cup dry white wine
3½ cups vegetable stock, heated
2 roasted red bell peppers, finely chopped
½ cup grated Parmesan cheese
1 cup finely chopped fresh basil leaves

salt and freshly ground black pepper
5 ounces fontina cheese, cut into cubes
⅓ cup all-purpose flour
2 large eggs, lightly beaten
⅔ cup fine dry breadcrumbs
vegetable oil, for deep-frying
piece of bread, to test vegetable oil

Heat half of the butter and the olive oil in a large, heavy-based saucepan over low–medium heat. Add the onion and garlic and sauté until softened. Add the rice, stirring to coat, and cook for 2 minutes, until translucent.

Pour in the wine and stir until all the liquid has been absorbed. Gradually add the stock, a ladle at a time. Make sure all the liquid is absorbed before the next addition. Cook for 20–25 minutes, stirring constantly, until all the liquid has been added and absorbed. The rice should be tender and cooked. Stir in the red bell peppers, Parmesan cheese, basil and the remaining butter. Season to taste. >

Line a tray with parchment (baking) paper and spread the risotto over. Set aside to cool.

Shape cooled risotto into balls the size of a small orange (*arancini* in Italian). Make a hole in each ball with your finger and insert a cube of fontina. Reshape ball to enclose cheese. Coat the arancini, rolling each one in flour, followed by the egg and then the crumbs.

Half-fill a large heavy-based saucepan with vegetable oil. Heat the vegetable oil to 350°F or until a piece of bread browns in 15 seconds when tested.

Fry the arancini in batches for 4–5 minutes, turning occasionally, until golden-brown. Remove using a slotted spoon and drain on paper towels. Season with salt.

Serve warm or at room temperature.

Stuffed Olives

MAKES 40 (SERVES 8–10)

40 large green olives, such as Gordal (Jumbo or Queen), pitted

½ cup all-purpose flour

2 large eggs, lightly beaten

1½ cups bread crumbs, made from day-old country-style bread

olive oil, for deep-frying

piece of bread, to test olive oil

FILLING

4½ ounces minced veal

4½ ounces minced pork

2 tablespoons finely grated Parmesan cheese

2 tablespoons finely grated provolone

2 tablespoons finely diced onion

1 teaspoon finely chopped fresh rosemary

½ clove garlic, finely chopped

½ teaspoon finely grated lemon zest

salt and freshly ground black pepper

To make the filling, combine all of the ingredients together in a medium bowl. Season with salt and pepper. Spoon the filling into a pastry bag fitted with a small plain nozzle and pipe into the olives.

Coat the olives, rolling each one in flour, followed by egg and then crumbs. Half-fill a heavy-based saucepan with olive oil. Heat the olive oil to 350°F or until a piece of bread browns in 15 seconds when tested. Fry the olives in batches for 2–3 minutes, turning occasionally, until golden-brown. Remove using a slotted spoon and drain on paper towels.

Soups

Italian soups vary from delicate broths such as stracciatella, to hearty vegetable, bean and pasta-filled soups, such as the well-known minestrone.

Often accompanied with crusty bread, soups can stand alone as a satisfying meal, or can be served as the first course of a traditional Italian meal. For best results, always use homemade or quality stock.

❮ FENNEL, TOMATO & SAUSAGE SOUP (PAGE 28)

Fennel, Tomato & Sausage Soup

SERVES 4

4 tablespoons olive oil

4 spicy Italian sausages, casings
removed and meat sliced

2½ ounces diced pancetta

1 large onion, diced

3 cloves garlic, sliced

2 bay leaves

8 sprigs fresh thyme

1 large fennel bulb, trimmed
and thinly sliced

1 teaspoon soft brown sugar

3 pounds 5 ounces Roma
tomatoes, coarsely chopped

1 quart 2 fluid ounces chicken
stock

salt and freshly ground black
pepper

Heat half of the olive oil in a heavy-based saucepan over medium–high heat. Add the sausage meat and pancetta and cook until browned. Transfer to a plate and set aside.

Heat the remaining olive oil in the pan over low–medium heat. Add the onion, garlic, bay leaves and thyme, and sauté until golden. Add the fennel and sauté for 5 minutes, until just softened. Add the brown sugar and sauté, stirring, an additional 5 minutes, until golden-brown. Return the sausage and pancetta to the pan. Add the tomatoes and stock and bring to a boil. Decrease the heat and gently simmer for 20–30 minutes. Season with salt and pepper.

Minestrone

2 tablespoons olive oil
1 medium onion, diced
1¾ ounces pancetta, finely
    chopped
2 cloves garlic, finely chopped
1 stick celery, diced
1 medium carrot, diced
2 medium potatoes, peeled
    and diced
1 bay leaf
1 cup passata
2 tablespoons tomato paste
2 pints 10 fluid ounces chicken
    or vegetable stock
1 (14-ounce) can borlotti
    (Roman or Cranberry)
    beans, drained and rinsed
1 cup small pasta
1 medium zucchini, diced
¼ savoy cabbage, chopped
¼ cup chopped flat-leaf parsley
salt and freshly ground pepper
extra-virgin olive oil, to serve
grated Parmesan cheese, to
    serve

Heat the olive oil in a large, heavy-based saucepan over low–medium heat. Add the onion, pancetta and garlic and sauté until golden. Add celery, carrot and potato and cook for 3–4 minutes, until they begin to color. Add the bay leaf, passata, tomato paste and stock and bring to a boil. Add the beans, pasta, zucchini and cabbage, decrease the heat to low and gently simmer for 30–35 minutes, until the pasta and vegetables are cooked. Stir in the parsley and season with salt and pepper.

Serve drizzled with extra-virgin olive oil and scattered with Parmesan cheese.

ॐ Pancetta is Italian bacon. Passata is a sauce made with tomatoes, basil and water. Tomato puree, tomato sauce, or canned, drained tomatoes can substitue

Pasta & Bean Soup
Pasta e fagioli

SERVES 6

10½ ounces dried cannellini
    beans, soaked in cold water
    overnight
1 tablespoon salt
3 tablespoons olive oil
1 medium onion, finely
    chopped
1 stalk celery, finely chopped
2 cloves garlic, finely chopped
2 bay leaves
7 ounces pancetta, diced

2 pints 10 fluid ounces chicken
    or vegetable stock
1½ cups passata
juice of ½ lemon
5 ounces pappardelle (broad
    ribbon-shaped pasta),
    broken into shorter lengths
¼ cup chopped fresh flat-leaf
    parsley
salt and freshly ground pepper
extra-virgin olive oil, to serve

Bring a large saucepan of water to a boil. Add the drained beans, decrease the heat and gently simmer. Cook for 30 minutes. Add salt and cook an additional 30 minutes, until beans are al dente (firm, but not hard). Drain and set aside.

Heat the olive oil in a large saucepan over low–medium heat. Add the onion, celery, garlic and bay leaves and sauté until softened. Add the pancetta and cook an additional 3–5 minutes, until golden. Add the beans, stock, passata and lemon juice and bring to a boil. Add the pasta and cook for 10 minutes, until al dente. Stir in the parsley and season with salt and pepper.

Mussel & Clam Soup

Zuppa di cozze e vongole

SERVES 6

1 pound 2 ounces black
  mussels
1 pound 2 ounces clams
4 medium vine-ripened
  tomatoes, blanched and
  peeled
3 tablespoons extra-virgin
  olive oil
1 small onion, finely chopped

2 cloves garlic, finely chopped
½ cup dry white wine
1½ cups fish stock
¼ cup finely chopped fresh
  flat-leaf parsley
1½ tablespoons butter, diced
salt and freshly ground black
  pepper
4 slices ciabatta (Italian white)

bread, toasted

Scrub the mussels and clams clean, discarding any shells that remain open. Beard the mussels and rinse clean.

Cut the tomatoes into quarters. Scrape out the seeds and discard. Dice the flesh and set aside.

Heat the olive oil in a medium, heavy-based saucepan over low–medium heat. Add the onion and garlic, and sauté until softened. Pour in the wine and cook until reduced by half. Pour in the stock and bring to a boil. Decrease the heat and gently simmer for 10 minutes.

Add the tomatoes, mussels and clams. Cover and cook for 5 minutes, until shellfish have opened. (Discard any unopened shells.) Add the parsley and butter and toss to coat. Season with salt and pepper.

To serve, place a slice of bread in the bottom of each bowl and ladle the soup over.

Re-boiled Soup
Ribollita

SERVES 4–6

4 medium vine-ripened
  tomatoes, blanched and
  peeled
4 tablespoons olive oil
1 medium red onion, diced
1 leek, white part only,
  coarsely chopped
2 cloves garlic, finely chopped
2 stalks celery, diced
1 medium carrot, diced
1 medium potato, peeled and
  diced

1 (14-ounce) can cannellini
  beans, rinsed and drained
10½ ounces cavolo nero, stalks
  trimmed and leaves finely
  chopped
1⅓ quarts chicken stock
4 slices day-old ciabatta bread,
  to serve
grated parmesan, to serve
extra-virgin olive oil, to serve

Coarsely chop the tomatoes and set aside.

Heat 3 tablespoons of the olive oil in a large, heavy-based saucepan over low–medium heat. Add the onion, leek and garlic, and sauté until softened. Add the celery, carrot and potato, and cook for 5 minutes.

Add the tomato, beans and cavolo nero. Pour in the stock and bring to a boil. Decrease the heat to low, and gently simmer for 1–1½ hours, until the vegetables begin to fall apart. >

Preheat grill or broiler to medium. Brush the bread with the remaining olive oil and grill until golden-brown.

To serve, place a slice of bread in the bottom of each bowl and ladle the soup over. Top with Parmesan cheese and drizzle with extra-virgin olive oil.

☞ Cavolo nero is black leaf kale. Spinach, chard or other deep leafy greens can substitute.

Stracciatella

SERVES 6

1¼ quarts chicken or beef
   stock
½ cup risoni
salt and freshly ground black
   pepper
4 large eggs, lightly beaten
4 tablespoons grated Parmesan
   cheese
¼ cup finely chopped fresh
   flat-leaf parsley

Place the stock in a medium saucepan over medium–high heat and bring to a
boil. Add the risoni and cook for 10 minutes, until al dente. Season with salt
and pepper.

Pour the egg mixture into the soup in a thin stream, creating thin strands of
cooked egg. Cook an additional 1–2 minutes.

Serve sprinkled with Parmesan cheese and parsley.

o Risoni is pasta that looks like rice. It is often called orzo.

Wild Mushroom Soup

SERVES 4

10½ ounces assorted wild mushrooms, sliced if large

4 leaves cavolo nero, finely shredded

salt and freshly ground black pepper

extra-virgin olive oil, to serve

MUSHROOM STOCK

1 small onion, coarsely chopped

1 small carrot, coarsely chopped

2 stalks celery, coarsely chopped

1 ounces dried porcini mushrooms

2 bay leaves

4 stalks fresh parsley

3 sprigs fesh thyme

3 strips lemon zest

3 black peppercorns

1 clove garlic, crushed

1⅔ quarts water

To make the mushroom stock, place all the ingredients in a large pot over medium–high heat and bring to a boil. Decrease the heat to low and gently simmer for 2 hours, until the flavor is well-developed. Strain through a fine mesh sieve into a medium saucepan.

Add the mushrooms and cavolo nero to the pan and gently simmer for 5–10 minutes, until tender. Season with salt and pepper.

Serve drizzled with extra-virgin oil.

Potato & Roast Garlic Soup

SERVES 4

4 garlic bulbs
3 tablespoons olive oil
1 medium onion, diced
3 tablespoons finely chopped
    fresh thyme
2 bay leaves

3 medium potatoes, peeled
    and diced
1⅓ quarts chicken or vegetable
    stock
salt and freshly ground black
    pepper
white truffle oil, to serve

Preheat the oven to 350°F.

Wrap the garlic bulbs in aluminum foil and bake in the oven for 20–25 minutes.
Remove from the oven and remove skin when cooled.

Heat the olive oil in a large, heavy-based saucepan over low–medium heat. Add the
onion, thyme and bay leaves, and sauté until softened. Add the potatoes and stir for
3–4 minutes. Pour in the stock and bring to a boil. Decrease heat to low, add garlic
and gently simmer for 30–35 minutes, until potatoes are tender.

Remove from heat and let cool slightly. Using a food processor or blender, purée
until smooth. Return to the pan and reheat if necessary. Season with salt.

Serve with a drizzle of white truffle oil and freshly ground black pepper.

Tomato & Bread Soup

Pappa al pomodoro

SERVES 4

1 pound 6 ounces vine-ripened tomatoes, blanched and peeled
2 tablespoons olive oil
1 small onion, finely diced
1 clove garlic, finely chopped
1 stalk celery, finely diced
1⅓ quarts chicken or vegetable stock

2 thick slices day-old ciabatta bread, crusts removed and cubed
salt and freshly ground black pepper
3 tablespoons finely chopped fresh basil
shaved Parmesan cheese, to serve

Chop the tomatoes coarsely and set aside.

Heat the olive oil in a medium, heavy-based saucepan over low–medium heat. Add the onion, garlic and celery, and sauté until softened. Add the tomatoes and stock, and bring to a boil. Decrease the heat to low and gently simmer for 30 minutes. Add the bread, cover and cook an additional 10 minutes, until thickened. Season with salt and pepper.

Serve sprinkled with basil and Parmesan cheese.

Pea & Fennel Soup

SERVES 4

3 medium fennel bulbs
3 tablespoons olive oil
1 large onion, finely sliced
1⅔ quarts chicken stock
1 pound 2 ounces frozen peas

3 tablespoons chopped fresh
   dill
salt and freshly ground black
   pepper
4 thin slices salted ricotta
extra-virgin olive oil, to serve

Remove and discard the tough outer layers of the fennel. Cut bulbs in half lengthwise, remove the hard core, then finely slice.

Heat the olive oil in a heavy-based saucepan over low–medium heat. Add the onion and sauté until softened. Add the fennel and sauté an additional 5 minutes. Pour in the stock and bring to a boil. Decrease the heat to low and gently simmer for 20–25 minutes, until fennel is tender. Add the peas and cook an additional 5 minutes. Stir in the dill and season with salt and pepper.

Serve topped with salted ricotta and a drizzle of extra-virgin olive oil.

Pasta & Risotto

In Italy, pasta and risotto are traditionally served as the *primo piatto* or 'first plate'. The flavors are kept simple and a bowl of Parmesan cheese is always close at hand. Both pasta and risotto are highly adaptable and dishes require only a handful of ingredients. Always use quality stock, olive oil and cheeses for the best outcome. Pasta and risotto should be cooked until al dente—soft on the outside but still slightly firm to the tooth.

Fresh pasta is not necessarily superior to dried, nor is one variety better than another. Flat and thin pastas are designed to be coated in thinner sauces, whereas pasta shapes are designed to hold thicker sauces in their holes and ridges. Pastas with a rough surface will grip the sauce better than those with a smooth surface.

For best results cook pasta in a large pot of rapidly boiling salted water. (The pasta should be able to move around freely, to prevent sticking.)

‹ FRESH EGG PASTA (PAGE 48)

Rolling and Cutting Homemade Pasta

Pasta sheets Divide the prepared dough into quarters. Lightly flour the counter top and shape one portion into a small rectangle. Keep the remaining pieces covered in food wrap, to prevent drying out. Starting at the thickest setting, feed the dough through a pasta machine. Fold the sheet in three, to form a thick rectangle. Turn it 90 degrees and pass through the same setting 2–3 more times, until the dough becomes silky. Gradually work down the settings, dusting the dough occasionally with flour, until the desired thickness is reached. Cut the pasta sheet in half as it gets longer, to make it more manageable to work with.

Fettuccine Fix the appropriate attachment to your pasta machine. Trim the edges of the pasta sheets (above), lightly dust with flour and feed through the machine.

If cutting by hand, dust the pasta sheets with flour and roll up lengthwise. Cut into ⅜-inch widths and unravel.

To dry, drape the fettuccine over a wooden rod or rolling pin for 1–2 days, until completely dry. Pasta can then be stored in an airtight container for up to two months.

If cooking the pasta fresh, put it on a tray lined with a lightly floured kitchen towel or twist it into bundles until required.

Pappardelle Trim the edges of the pasta sheets (page 46), lightly dust with flour and roll up lengthwise. Cut into 1-inch widths and unravel. Dry or store as described above.

Lasagne sheets Trim the edges of the pasta sheets (page 46) and cut out 4-inch × 5-inch rectangles. Lay flat on an drying rack to dry for 1–2 days, until completely dry, or (if using fresh) put them on a tray lined with a lightly floured kitchen towel until needed.

Fresh Egg Pasta

SERVES 4 (5 OUNCES PER PORTION)

2²/₃ cups all-purpose flour
2 teaspoons salt
4 large eggs plus 2 large egg
   yolks, lightly beaten

Combine the flour and salt in a pile on a clean counter top. Make a well in the center and pour in the egg mixture. Work the egg into the flour, stirring with a fork, until dough begins to form. Knead the dough for 10–15 minutes, until it becomes soft, smooth and elastic. If the dough seems too sticky, add a little more flour; if too dry, wet your hands and knead in some water. Shape into a ball, cover with food wrap and refrigerate for 1 hour before rolling out.

🕭 Dough can be wrapped in food wrap and frozen for up to 3 months. Fresh pasta is best cooked and prepared on the same day.

Fresh Spinach Pasta
Pasta verde

SERVES 4 (5 OUNCES PER PORTION)

10 ounces spinach leaves
water, to blanch spinach
2 cups all-purpose flour
2 teaspoons salt
1 large egg plus 4 large egg
   yolks, lightly beaten

Place a large saucepan of water over high heat and bring to a boil. Blanch the spinach for 10 seconds, until wilted. Drain and squeeze out as much moisture as possible. Finely chop and set aside.

Combine the flour and salt in a pile on a clean counter top. Make a well in the center, pour in the egg mixture and add the spinach. Work the egg and spinach into the flour, stirring with a fork, until dough begins to form. Knead the dough for 10–15 minutes, until it becomes soft, smooth and elastic. If the dough seems too sticky, add a little more flour; if too dry, wet your hands and knead in some water. Shape into a ball, cover with food wrap and refrigerate for 1 hour before rolling out.

꙰ Dough can be wrapped in food wrap and frozen for up to 3 months.

Bucatini with Spicy Tomato Sauce
Bucatini Amatriciana

SERVES 4

2 tablespoons olive oil

7 ounces pancetta, finely sliced

1 medium red onion, sliced

2 cloves garlic, thinly sliced

1 long red chili pepper, sliced

1 tablespoon finely chopped
fresh rosemary

¼ cup red wine

6 large ripe tomatoes, diced

salt and freshly ground black
pepper

1 pound 2 ounces bucatini
(hollow pasta rods)

water, salt and olive oil, to cook
bucatini

1 cup grated Pecorino cheese

Heat the olive oil in a large, heavy-based saucepan over low–medium heat.
Add the pancetta and cook for 5 minutes, until crisp. Decrease the heat to low,
add the onion, garlic, chilli and rosemary and sauté, stirring occasionally, for 10
minutes, until caramelized. Add the wine and tomatoes and gently simmer for
15 minutes, until softened to a chunky sauce consistency. Season with salt
and pepper.

Meanwhile bring a large pot of water to a boil. Add a tablespoon of salt and a
splash of olive oil. Cook the pasta according to the package directions, until al
dente. Drain and return to the pan.

Pour sauce over the pasta and toss to combine. Serve scattered with Pecorino
cheese.

Chicken & Mushroom Tortellini with Cream Sauce

SERVES 4

1 quantity fresh egg pasta
dough (page 48)
all-purpose flour, to dust
dough
water, salt and oil to cook the
tortellini
1 beaten egg, for brushing
1 cup freshly grated Parmesan
cheese

1 cup finely grated Parmesan
cheese
¼ cup cream
2 large eggs, lightly beaten
1 clove garlic, crushed
2 tablespoons finely chopped
fresh oregano
salt and freshly ground black
pepper

FILLING
½ ounce dried porcini
mushrooms, soaked in
warm water for 15 minutes
10½ ounces minced chicken

SAUCE
1 cup cream
5 ounces mascarpone (Italian
cream cheese)

To make the filling, drain and finely chop the porcini mushrooms and place in a medium bowl. Add the chicken, Parmesan cheese, cream, egg, garlic and oregano and stir to combine. Season with salt and pepper. Cover with food wrap and refrigerate until required.

To make the tortellini, divide the pasta dough into quarters. Lightly flour the counter top and shape one portion into a small rectangle. >

Keep the remaining pieces covered in food wrap, to prevent drying out. Feed the dough through a pasta machine, starting at the thickest setting. Fold the sheet in three to form a thick rectangle. Turn it 90 degrees and pass through the same setting 2–3 more times, until the dough becomes silky.

Gradually work down the settings, dusting the dough occasionally with flour, until the desired thickness is reached. Cut the pasta sheet in half as it gets longer to make it more manageable.

Bring a large pot of water to a boil. Add a tablespoon of salt and a splash of olive oil.

Trim each pasta sheet and cut out eight 4-inch squares. Place a spoonful of filling in the center of each square. Brush the edges with egg and fold the pasta over the filling to create a triangular shape and press to seal. Wrap each tortellini around your finger, crossing the two points over in the center. Press to seal and place on a lightly floured kitchen towel.

To make the sauce, pour the cream into a large fry pan over medium heat. Bring to a boil and gently simmer for 3–5 minutes, or until thickened slightly. Add the mascarpone and stir to combine.

In rapidly boiling water, cook the tortellini in batches for 4–5 minutes, until floating and al dente. Remove tortellini using a slotted spoon and drain over the pot. Add the tortellini to the prepared sauce and toss to coat. Serve topped with Parmesan cheese.

Gnocchi alla Romana

1 quart 2 fluid ounces milk
1 cup semolina (large grains of
    wheat)
1½ cups grated Parmesan
    cheese

3 large egg yolks
4 tablespoons butter, cubed
salt
butter or oil, to prepare baking
    sheet and ovenproof dish

Place the milk in a medium saucepan over low–medium heat and bring almost to boiling point. Decrease the heat to low and gradually pour in the semolina, stirring. Cook for 10–15 minutes, stirring continuously, until semolina thickens and comes away from the sides of the pan.

Remove from heat and stir in half of the Parmesan cheese, the egg yolks and the butter. Season with salt. Pour onto a lightly greased baking sheet to about ⅜-inch thick, cover with parchment (baking) paper and refrigerate for 1 hour, or until firm.

Preheat the oven to 400°F. Grease an 7-inch × 10-inch ovenproof dish.

Cut rounds out of the set semolina using a 2-inch biscuit cutter. Arrange the rounds, overlapping slightly, in greased dish. Sprinkle with the remaining Parmesan cheese and bake for 15–20 minutes, until golden-brown.

Pumpkin, Spinach & Pine Nut Cannelloni

SERVES 6–8

2 (7-ounce) packages dried
  cannelloni tubes
5 ounces mozzarella, thinly
  sliced

FILLING
1 pound 7 ounces pumpkin,
  skinned, deseeded and cut
  into 1-inch cubes
1 tablespoon olive oil
10½ ounces spinach leaves
water, to blanch the spinach
1 pound 5 ounces ricotta
2 cups grated Parmesan cheese
1 cup fresh basil, finely
  chopped
½ cup pine nuts, lightly
  toasted and coarsely
  chopped

3 cloves garlic, crushed
1½ teaspoons ground nutmeg
salt and freshly ground pepper

TOMATO SAUCE
4 tablespoons olive oil
1 large onion, finely chopped
3 cloves garlic, finely chopped
2 (1 pound 12-ounce) cans
  whole peeled tomatoes,
  coarsely chopped
½ cup water
½ cup chopped fresh oregano
  leaves
2 tablespoons tomato paste
1 tablespoon sugar
salt and freshly ground black
  pepper

Preheat the oven to 350°F. Grease a 9-inch × 13-inch baking dish.

Spread pumpkin on a large baking sheet. Drizzle with olive oil and toss to coat. Bake in preheated oven for 30–40 minutes, until softened and golden-brown. Remove from the oven, mash and set aside to cool. (Leave oven on.)

To make the sauce, heat the olive oil in a medium, heavy-based saucepan over low–medium heat. Add the onion and garlic, and sauté until softened. Add the tomatoes, water, oregano, tomato paste and sugar, and stir to combine. Gently simmer for 30 minutes. Season with salt and pepper and set aside.

Place a large saucepan of water over high heat and bring to a boil. Blanch the spinach for 10 seconds, until wilted. Drain and squeeze out as much moisture as possible. Finely chop and place in a large bowl. Add the pumpkin, ricotta, Parmesan cheese, basil, pine nuts, garlic and nutmeg. Stir to combine and season with salt and pepper.

Spoon the pumpkin mixture into a pastry bag fitted with a large plain nozzle. Fill the cannelloni tubes with the mixture and place in a single layer in the prepared baking dish. Pour the tomato sauce over and scatter with mozzarella. Cover with aluminum foil and bake for 30 minutes. Remove the foil and bake an additional 10 minutes, until golden-brown.

Potato, Mint & Goat Cheese Agnolotti with Lemon Butter

SERVES 4

1 quantity fresh spinach pasta
   dough (page 49)
all-purpose flour, to dust
   dough
water, salt and oil, to cook
   agnolotti
1 beaten egg, for brushing
Parmesan cheese, to serve

7 ounces soft goat cheese,
   crumbled
7 ounces ricotta cheese,
   crumbled
4 tablespoons finely chopped
   fresh mint
salt and freshly ground black
   pepper

FILLING
10½ ounces potatoes
cold water, to cook potatoes

LEMON BUTTER
7 tablespoons butter
juice of ½ lemon

To make the filling, place the potatoes in a medium saucepan, cover with cold water and bring to a boil. Decrease the heat and simmer for 20–30 minutes, until potatoes are tender. Drain.

Peel the potatoes while still warm and pass through a potato ricer or mash using a potato masher. Place the potatoes, goat cheese, ricotta and mint in a medium bowl and stir to combine. Season with salt and pepper. Cover with food wrap and refrigerate until required. >

To make the agnolotti, divide the pasta dough into quarters. Lightly flour the counter top and shape one portion into a small rectangle. Keep the remaining pieces covered in food wrap, to prevent drying out.

Feed the dough through a pasta machine, starting at the thickest setting. Fold the sheet in three, to form a thick rectangle. Turn it 90 degrees and pass through the same setting 2–3 more times, until dough becomes silky. Gradually work down the settings, dusting the dough occasionally with flour, until the desired thickness is reached. Cut the pasta sheet in half as it gets longer, to make it more manageable.

Trim the pasta sheets and cut out 3-inch rounds using a fluted dough wheel. Place a spoonful of filling in the center of each round. Brush the edges with egg and fold the pasta over the filling to create a crescent shape. Press around the filling to seal and remove any trapped air. Place onto a lightly floured kitchen towel.

Bring a large pot of water to a boil. Add salt and a splash of olive oil. Cook the agnolotti in rapidly boiling water in batches, for 4–5 minutes, until floating and al dente. Remove agnolotti using a slotted spoon, drain over the pot and transfer to serving plates or bowls.

Melt the butter in a small heavy-based fry pan over low–medium heat. When it begins to bubble, squeeze in the lemon juice. Pour sauce over the agnolotti and top with Parmesan cheese and freshly ground pepper.

✆ Agnolotti are small crecent-shaped stuffed pasta, similar to ravioli.

Spaghetti Vongole

SERVES 4

1 pound 5 ounces fresh or
   1 pound 2 ounces dried
   spaghetti
water, salt and oil, to cook
   spaghetti
4 tablespoons extra-virgin
   olive oil
1 medium onion, finely diced
2 cloves garlic, finely chopped
1 large red chili pepper,
   deseeded and finely chopped

½ cup dry white wine
2 pound 3 ounces small clams,
   washed (discard any shells
   that stay open)
½ cup chopped fresh flat-leaf
   parsley
juice of ½ lemon
salt and freshly ground black
   pepper

Bring a large pot of water to a boil. Add a tablespoon of salt and a splash of olive oil. Cook the pasta for 3–4 minutes if fresh, or if dried, until al dente. Drain and return to the pan.

Heat the olive oil in a large, heavy-based saucepan over low–medium heat. Add the onion, garlic and chili pepper, and sauté until softened. Increase the heat to medium, pour in the wine and add the clams. Cover and cook, shaking occasionally, for 5 minutes, until most of the shells have opened. Discard any unopened shells. Add the parsley and lemon juice and stir to combine. Season with salt and pepper.

Transfer pasta to the pan with the clams and toss to combine.

Penne with Sausage & Spicy Tomato Sauce

SERVES 4

1 pound 5 ounces fresh or
   1 pound 2 ounces dried
   penne
3 tablespoons olive oil
1 medium onion, sliced
3 cloves garlic, finely chopped
4 Italian sausages, casings
   removed and meat crumbled
½ cup red wine

1 (1 pound 12-ounce) can
   whole peeled tomatoes,
   chopped
2 dried red chili peppers,
   crumbled
salt and freshly ground black
   pepper

Bring a large pot of water to a boil. Add a tablespoon of salt and a splash of oil. Cook the pasta for 3–4 minutes if fresh or according to the package directions if dried, until al dente. Drain and return to the pot.

Heat the olive oil in a medium, heavy-based saucepan over low–medium heat. Add the onion and garlic, and sauté until softened. Increase the heat to medium. Add the sausage meat, stirring to break up, and cook for 5 minutes, until browned. Pour in the wine and cook until reduced by half. Add the tomato and chili peppers, and bring to a boil. Decrease the heat to low and gently simmer for 15 minutes, until flavors have developed. Season with salt and pepper. Add the pasta and toss to combine.

Beet & Taleggio Ravioli

SERVES 4

all-purpose flour, to dust
    dough
1 quantity fresh egg pasta
    dough (page 48)
water, salt and oil, to cook
    ravioli
1 beaten egg, for brushing
7 tablespoons butter
½ cup finely grated Parmesan
    cheese

FILLING
2 medium beets (about 10½
    ounces each)
7 ounces ricotta cheese
½ cup ground almond meal
3½ ounces taleggio cheese,
    finely chopped
salt and freshly ground black
    pepper
1 large egg, lightly beaten

Preheat the oven to 400°F.

To make the filling, wrap each beet in aluminum foil and place on baking sheet. Bake in the oven for 45–60 minutes, until tender. Set aside to cool slightly. Peel using a small knife and chop coarsely. Place in a food processor or blender and blend until smooth. Add the ricotta cheese, ground almond meal and taleggio and blend until combined. Season with salt and pepper. Cover with food wrap and refrigerate until needed.

To make the ravioli, divide the pasta dough into quarters. Lightly flour the counter top and shape one portion into a small rectangle. Keep the remaining pieces covered in food wrap, to prevent drying out. Feed the dough through a pasta machine, starting at the thickest setting. Fold the sheet in three, to form a thick rectangle. Turn it 90 degrees and pass through the same setting 2–3 more times, until the dough becomes silky. Gradually work down the settings, dusting the dough occasionally with flour, until the desired thickness is reached. Cut the pasta sheet in half as it gets longer, to make it more manageable.

Bring a large pot of water to a boil. Add a tablespoon of salt and a splash of oil.

Trim each pasta sheet into two even lengths. On one of the pasta sheets, place spoonfuls of filling in two even rows of five. Brush egg around the filling. Place a second sheet of pasta over the top, pressing around the filling to seal and remove any trapped air. Cut out the ravioli using a fluted dough wheel. Place ravioli onto a lightly floured kitchen towel. Repeat the process with the remaining dough and filling.

When the water is boiling rapidly, cook the ravioli in batches for 4–5 minutes, until floating and al dente. Remove ravioli using a slotted spoon, drain over the pot and transfer to serving plates or bowls.

Melt the butter in a medium fry pan over low heat. Pour it over the ravioli and scatter with Parmesan cheese.

∂ Taleggio is a semi-soft, washed-rind pungent Italian cheese. Substitute Fontina or Bel Paese for less pungency.

Farfalle with Tuna, Capers & Arugula

SERVES 4

water, salt and oil, to cook
  farfalle
1 pound 2 ounces farfalle
  (bow-tie pasta)
¼ cup extra-virgin olive oil
1 small red onion, sliced
2 cloves garlic, finely chopped
finely grated zest and juice of
  1 lemon

1 (15-ounce) can good-quality
  tuna in olive oil, drained
  and flaked
3 ounces wild arugula
1 tablespoon baby capers,
  rinsed
salt and freshly ground black
  pepper

Bring a large pot of water to a boil. Add a tablespoon of salt and a splash of oil. Cook the pasta until al dente. Drain and return to the pot.

Heat the olive oil in a large fry pan over low–medium heat. Add the onion, garlic and lemon zest and sauté until softened. Add lemon juice, tuna, arugula and capers and toss to combine. Season with salt and pepper.

Add tuna mixture to the pasta and toss to combine.

Lasagna Bolognese

SERVES 6–8

2 (9-ounce) packages dried
  lasagna sheets
1 cup grated Parmesan cheese

BOLOGNESE SAUCE
2 tablespoons extra-virgin
  olive oil
1 large onion, finely diced
2 cloves garlic, finely chopped
1 small carrot, finely diced
1 stalk celery, finely diced
10½ ounces minced pork
10½ ounces minced veal
½ cup red wine
1 (14-ounce) can diced
  tomatoes
2 cups passata
3 tablespoons tomato paste

2 tablespoons finely chopped
  fresh oregano
3 bay leaves
1 teaspoon sugar
¼ teaspoon ground cinnamon
¼ teaspoon ground nutmeg
salt and freshly ground pepper

BÉCHAMEL SAUCE
1 quart 2 fluid ounces milk
1 bay leaf
2 cloves
4 tablespoons butter
4 tablespoons all-purpose
  flour
pinch of ground nutmeg
salt and white pepper

To make the bolognese sauce, heat the olive oil in a large, heavy-based saucepan over low–medium heat. Add the onion and garlic, and sauté until golden. Add the carrot and celery, and sauté for 5 minutes, or until just softened. Increase the heat to medium, add the miced pork and veal and cook for 5 minutes, stirring to break up, until browned. Pour in the wine and cook until reduced by half. Add the tomatoes, passata, tomato paste, oregano, bay leaves, sugar, cinnamon and nutmeg. Stir to combine and bring to a boil. Decrease the heat to low and gently simmer for 45 minutes, until thick. Season with salt and pepper.

Preheat the oven to 350°F. Lightly grease a deep 9-inch × 13-inch ovenproof dish.

To make the béchamel sauce, place milk, bay leaf and cloves in a saucepan and bring a boil. Remove from heat and set aside to infuse.

Melt the butter in a medium saucepan over low heat. Add the flour and cook, stirring with a wooden spoon, for 1–2 minutes. Gradually add the milk, discarding the bay leaf and cloves, and stir until smooth. Gently simmer, stirring constantly, for 5–10 minutes until thickened. Season with nutmeg, salt and white pepper. Remove from heat and cover the surface with a piece of parchment (baking) paper, to prevent a skin from forming. Set aside.

Spread a thin layer of meat sauce over the bottom of the prepared dish and lay lasagna sheets over the top. Spread a layer of meat on top, followed by a layer of béchamel sauce. Continue the layers, finishing with the béchamel sauce. Sprinkle with Parmesan cheese. Bake for 35–40 minutes, until pasta is cooked and the top is golden-brown.

Spaghetti with Prawns & Saffron Cream

SERVES 4

water, salt and oil, to cook
   spaghetti
1 pound 5 ounces fresh or
   1 pound 2 ounces dried
   spaghetti
2 tablespoons extra-virgin olive oil
14 ounces raw (green) prawns,
   shelled, deveined with tails
   left on

1 clove garlic, crushed
1 dried red chili pepper, deseeded
   and finely chopped
$1/3$ cup dry white wine
1 teaspoon saffron threads,
   soaked in $1/3$ cup warm water
1 cup cream
salt and freshly ground pepper

Bring a large pot of water to a boil. Add a tablespoon of salt and a splash of olive oil. Cook the pasta for 3–4 minutes if fresh, or if dried, until al dente. Drain and return to the pan.

Meanwhile, heat the olive oil in a large fry pan over low–medium heat. Add the prawns and cook for 1 minute on each side, until they change color. Remove from the pan and set aside.

Add the garlic and red chili pepper to the pan and sauté until softened. Pour in the wine, saffron and its liquid and cook until reduced by half. Pour in the cream and bring to a boil. Decrease the heat to low and gently simmer for 5 minutes, until thickened slightly. Return the prawns to the pan and season with salt and pepper. Add the pasta and toss to coat.

Capelli with Sardines & Garlic Breadcrumbs

SERVES 4

5 tablespoons extra-virgin olive oil

4 cloves garlic, finely chopped

2 cups breadcrumbs, from day-old country-style bread

1 pound 2 ounces capelli (thin rod-shaped pasta)

water, salt and oil, to cook capelli

1 pound 2 ounces fresh sardines, scaled and filleted

9 ounces cherry tomatoes, halved

4 tablespoons chopped fresh flat-leaf parsley

2 tablespoons pine nuts, lightly toasted

salt and freshly ground black pepper

Heat 2 tablespoons of the olive oil in a large fry pan over medium heat. Add the garlic and breadcrumbs and fry, stirring, for 5 minutes, until crisp and golden. Transfer to a plate and set aside.

Bring a large pot of water to a boil. Add a tablespoon of salt and a splash of olive oil. Cook the pasta until al dente. Drain and return to the pot.

Heat 2 tablespoons of olive oil in a fry pan over low–medium heat. Cook the sardines in batches, for 1–2 minutes, until cooked. Transfer to a plate and set aside. Heat remaining olive oil in the pan over low–medium heat. Cook tomatoes for 2–3 minutes, until just softened. Add the sardines, parsley, pine nuts and half the breadcrumbs and toss to combine. Season with salt and pepper. Serve over the pasta, topped with remaining breadcrumbs.

Potato Gnocchi with Napoli

SERVES 4

1 cup grated Parmesan cheese, to serve

NAPOLI SAUCE

3 tablespoons extra-virgin olive oil

1 medium onion, diced

1 clove garlic, sliced

1 small carrot, diced

1 stalk celery, diced

2 (14-ounce) cans whole peeled tomatoes, coarsely chopped

1 teaspoon sugar

⅓ cup finely chopped fresh basil

salt and freshly ground pepper

GNOCCHI

2 pound 3 ounces desirée (red-skinned) potatoes

cold water, to cook potatoes

1 large egg, lightly beaten

1 teaspoon salt

1¾ cups all-purpose flour, plus extra for dusting

water, salt and oil, to cook gnocchi

To make the sauce, heat the olive oil in a medium, heavy-based saucepan over low–medium heat. Add the onion and garlic, and sauté until softened. Add the carrot and celery, and sauté an additional 5 minutes. Add the tomatoes and sugar and bring to a boil. Decrease the heat to low and gently simmer for 45 minutes. Remove from heat and let cool slightly. Pour into a food processor or blender and blend until puréed. Return to the pan, stir in the basil and season with salt and pepper.

Preheat the oven to 300°F. Grease a medium-sized baking dish.

To make the gnocchi, place the potatoes in a large saucepan, cover with cold water and bring to a boil. Decrease the heat and simmer for 25–30 minutes, until tender. Drain. Peel the potatoes while still warm and mash. Pile the potatoes on a clean counter top and create a well in the middle. Add the egg, salt and two thirds of the flour. Mix until a dough begins to form. Add more flour as required and gently knead until just combined.

Divide the gnocchi dough into six portions and roll out into sausage lengths ⅜-inch in diameter. Cut into ¾-inch pieces and place on a tray lined with a lightly floured kitchen towel.

Reheat Napoli sauce and keep warm.

Bring a large pot of water to a boil. Add a tablespoon of salt and a splash of oil. Cook the gnocchi in batches, for 3–5 minutes, until they float to the surface. Remove gnocchi using a slotted spoon, drain over the pot and transfer to prepared dish. Place in the oven to keep warm, until the remaining gnocchi is cooked. Spoon sauce over gnocchi and top with Parmesan cheese.

> If not cooking immediately, gnocchi can be stored on a tray, wrapped in a clean lightly floured kitchen towel, at room temperature for a few hours. Do not refrigerate as gnocchi will discolor. Alternatively, gnocchi can be frozen. Lay the gnocchi on a tray and freeze until solid. Transfer to an airtight container or zip-lock bag and store in the freezer for up to one month.

Fettuccine Carbonara

SERVES 4

1 pound 5 ounces fresh or
   1 pound 2 ounces dried
   fettuccine (little ribbon
   pasta)
water, salt and oil, to cook
   fettuccine
2 tablespoons extra-virgin
   olive oil
2 tablespoons butter
7 ounces pancetta, thinly sliced

1 clove garlic, peeled and
   crushed
¼ cup cream
4 large egg yolks
1 cup grated Parmesan cheese
salt and freshly ground black
   pepper
2 tablespoons chopped fresh
   flat-leaf parsley, to serve

Bring a large pot of water to a boil. Add a tablespoon of salt and a splash of olive oil. Cook the pasta for 3–4 minutes if fresh, or if dried, until al dente. Drain and return to the pot.

Heat the oil and butter in a large fry pan over medium heat. Add the pancetta and garlic, and cook until crisp. Discard the garlic. Pour in the cream and simmer for 3–5 minutes, until thickened slightly. Add the pasta to the pan and toss to coat. Remove from the heat and stir in the egg yolks and Parmesan cheese. Season with salt and pepper.

Serve scattered with parsley.

Fettuccine Alfredo

SERVES 4

1 pound 5 ounces fresh or
    1 pound 2 ounces dried
    fettuccine
water, salt and oil, to cook
    fettuccine
7 tablespoons butter
1 cup cream

1¼ cups grated Parmesan
    cheese
2 tablespoons chopped flat-leaf
    parsley
salt and freshly ground black
    pepper

Bring a large pot of water to a boil. Add a tablespoon of salt and a splash of olive oil. Cook the pasta for 3–4 minutes if fresh, or if dried, until al dente. Drain and return to the pot.

Melt the butter in a medium fry pan over low–medium heat. Pour in the cream and bring to a boil. Decrease the heat to low and gently simmer for 5 minutes, or until thickened slightly. Add most of the Parmesan cheese and all of the parsley and stir to combine. Season with salt and pepper. Pour sauce over the pasta and toss to coat.

Serve topped with the remaining Parmesan cheese.

Pappardelle with Creamy Walnut Sauce

SERVES 4

1 pound 5 ounces fresh or
 1 pound 2 ounces dried
 pappardelle (broad, flat
 pasta ribbons)
water, salt and oil, to cook
 pappardelle
1 tablespoon extra-virgin olive oil
1 tablespoon butter
1 medium onion, finely
 chopped

2 cloves garlic, finely chopped
2 cups walnut halves, coarsely
 chopped
1 cup cream
5 ounces mascarpone
½ cup shaved Parmesan cheese
¼ cup fresh basil leaves, torn
salt and freshly ground black
 pepper

Bring a large pot of water to a boil. Add a tablespoon of salt and a splash of olive oil. Cook the pasta for 3–4 minutes if fresh, or if dried, until al dente. Drain and return to the pan.

Heat the extra-virgin olive oil and butter in a medium, heavy-based saucepan over low–medium heat. Add the onion and garlic, and sauté until softened. Add the walnuts and cook for 3–5 minutes, until golden-brown. Add the cream and simmer for 3–5 minutes until thickened slightly. Stir in the mascarpone, Parmesan cheese and basil. Season with salt and pepper.

Add the pasta to the sauce and toss to combine.

Eggplant Lasagna

SERVES 6–8

½ cup olive oil

1 large onion, finely diced

2 cloves garlic, finely chopped

2 (1 pound 12-ounce) cans whole peeled tomatoes, coarsely chopped

2 tablespoons tomato paste

1 tablespoon malt or cider vinegar

2 tablespoons finely chopped fresh oregano

2 tablespoons chopped fresh basil

1 teaspoon sugar

salt and freshly ground black pepper

4 large eggplants, trimmed and cut lengthwise into ³/₈-inch thick slices

2 (9-ounce) packages dried lasagna sheets

10½ onces provolone, grated

7 ounces buffalo mozzarella, torn

Heat 2 tablespoons of olive oil in a large, heavy-based saucepan over low–medium heat. Add the onion and garlic, and sauté until softened. Add the tomatoes, tomato paste, vinegar, herbs and sugar, and stir to combine. Gently simmer for 15–20 minutes, until thickened slightly and flavors have developed. Season with salt and pepper.

Preheat the oven to 350°F. Lightly grease a deep 9-inch × 13-inch ovenproof dish.

Place the eggplant slices and remaining olive oil in a large bowl and toss to coat. Heat a large fry pan over medium–high heat. Cook the eggplant slices for 1–2 minutes on each side, until golden-brown.

Spread a thin layer of sauce in the bottom of the prepared dish. Cover with a layer of the cooked eggplant and a sprinkling of provolone cheese, followed by a layer of sauce. Lay lasagna sheets over the top. Continue the layers, finishing with the sauce. Scatter with mozzarella and bake for 35–40 minutes, until pasta is cooked and the top is golden-brown.

Orecchiette with Broccoli, Tomato & Ricotta

SERVES 4

salted water, to cook broccoli
14 ounces broccoli, cut into
    florets
water, salt and oil, to cook
    orecchiette
1 pound 2 ounces orecchiette
    (small ear-shaped pasta)
4 tablespoons extra-virgin
    olive oil

2 cloves garlic, finely chopped
9 ounces cherry tomatoes
7 ounces ricotta, crumbled
salt and freshly ground black
    pepper
¼ cup grated Parmesan cheese

Bring a medium saucepan of salted water to a boil. Cook the broccoli for 3–4 minutes, until tender. Drain and set aside.

Bring a large pot of water to a boil. Add a tablespoon of salt and a splash of olive oil. Cook the pasta until al dente. Drain and return to the pot.

Heat the extra-virgin olive oil in a large fry pan over low–medium heat. Add the garlic and sauté until softened. Add the tomatoes and cook for 2 minutes, until just softened. Add the broccoli and cook an additional 1–2 minutes, until heated through. Add the ricotta and toss to combine. Season with salt and pepper. Add pasta and toss to coat. Serve topped with Parmesan cheese.

Pappardelle with Lamb Ragu

SERVES 4

3 tablespoons extra-virgin olive
   oil
1 medium onion, sliced
2 cloves garlic, finely chopped
14 ounces minced lamb
½ cup dry white wine
5 ripe tomatoes, diced
½ cup water
¼ cup chopped fresh flat-leaf
   parsley

2 bay leaves
salt and freshly ground black
   pepper
1 pound 5 ounces fresh or
   1 pound 2 ounces dried
   pappardelle
water, salt and oil, to cook
   pappardelle
1 cup grated Pecorino cheese

Heat the olive oil in a medium, heavy-based saucepan over low–medium heat. Add the onion and garlic, and sauté until golden. Increase the heat to medium. Add the minced lamb, stirring to break up, and cook for 5 minutes, until browned. Pour in the wine and cook until reduced by half. Add the tomatoes, water, parsley and bay leaves and bring to a boil. Decrease heat to low and simmer for 45 minutes, until thick and flavors have developed. Season with salt and pepper.

Bring a large pot of water to a boil. Add a tablespoon of salt and a splash of olive oil. Cook the pasta for 4–5 minutes if fresh, or if dried, until al dente. Drain and return to the pot. Spoon lamb ragu over the pasta to serve, and top with Pecorino cheese.

Trenette with Potatoes, Beans & Pesto

Trenette al pesto Genovese

SERVES 4

salted water, to cook potatoes and
green beans
4 new potatoes, peeled and cut
into ³/₈-inch slices
4½ ounces green beans, cut in
half
1 pound 2 ounces trenette (thin
ribbon-ridged pasta)
water, salt and oil, to cook trenette

BASIL PESTO
¼ cup pine nuts, lightly toasted
1 clove garlic, roughly chopped
¼ cup Parmesan cheese, grated
¼ cup extra-virgin olive oil
1½ cups fresh basil leaves
salt and freshly ground black pepper

Bring a saucepan of salted water to a boil. Cook the potatoes for 2 minutes, add
the beans and cook an additional 2 minutes. Drain and set aside.

Bring a large pot of water to a boil. Add a tablespoon of salt and a splash of olive oil.
Cook the pasta until al dente. Drain, reserving 4 tablespoons of the cooking water, and
return pasta to the pot.

To make the pesto, place the pine nuts and garlic in a food processor or blender and
blend for 5 seconds. Add the Parmesan cheese and half the olive oil and blend an
additional 5 seconds. Add the basil leaves and the remaining olive oil and blend until
a paste is formed. Season with salt and pepper. Transfer to a small bowl and stir in
the reserved cooking water.

Add the pesto, potato and beans to the pasta and toss to coat.

Herbed Tomato & Fontina Risotto

SERVES 4

6 tablespoons butter

1 tablespoon olive oil

1 medium onion, finely diced

1 clove garlic, finely chopped

1½ cups arborio or other risotto rice

2 (14½-ounce) cans chopped tomatoes

2 tablespoons finely chopped fresh sage

2 tablespoons finely chopped fresh rosemary

1 quart 2 fluid ounces vegetable stock, heated

½ cup grated Parmesan cheese

3 ounces fontina, cubed

2 tablespoons finely chopped fresh basil

salt and freshly ground black pepper

Heat half the butter and the olive oil in a large, heavy-based saucepan over low–medium heat. Add the onion and garlic, and sauté until softened. Add the rice, stirring to coat, and cook for 2 minutes, until translucent.

Add the tomatoes, sage and rosemary, and stir to combine. Gradually add the stock, a ladle at a time, stirring constantly. Make sure all the liquid is absorbed before the next addition. Cook for 20–25 minutes, adding the stock gradually and stirring continuously, until the rice is al dente. Stir in the Parmesan cheese and the remaining butter. Add the fontina and basil, stirring until the cheese melts. Season with salt and pepper.

Seared Scallop & Lemon Risotto

SERVES 4

3 tablespoons olive oil
1 pound 2 ounces scallops, roe
   removed
6 tablespoons butter
1 medium onion, finely diced
1 clove garlic, finely chopped
1 large red chili pepper,
   deseeded and finely chopped
finely grated zest and juice
   of 3 lemons

1½ cups arborio or other
   risotto rice
½ cup dry white wine
1 quart 10 fluid ounces fish
   stock, heated
4 tablespoons finely chopped
   fresh basil
salt and freshly ground black
   pepper

Heat 2 tablespoons of the olive oil in a large fry pan over medium–high heat.
Sear the scallops for 1–2 minutes on each side, until golden-brown and just
cooked through. Transfer to a plate and set aside.

Heat half the butter and the remaining olive oil in a large, heavy-based
saucepan over low–medium heat. Add the onion, garlic, red chili pepper and
lemon zest, and sauté until softened. Add the rice, stirring to coat, and cook for
2 minutes, until translucent. >

Pour in the wine and cook, stirring, until absorbed. Gradually add the stock, a ladle at a time, stirring constantly. Make sure most of the liquid is absorbed before the next addition. Cook for 20 minutes, then add the scallops and lemon juice and cook an additional 3–5 minutes, adding any additional stock if required, until the liquid has been absorbed and rice is al dente. Stir in the basil and the remaining butter. Season with salt and pepper.

Risotto Milanese

SERVES 4

4 tablespoons butter
2½ ounces veal or beef marrow
1 large onion, finely chopped
1 clove garlic, finely chopped
1½ cups arborio or other
    risotto rice
½ cup dry vermouth or white
    wine
1 teaspoon saffron threads,
    infused in 3 tablespoons hot
    water

1 quart 10 fluid ounces
    chicken or vegetable stock,
    heated
½ cup grated Parmesan cheese
salt and freshly ground black
    pepper
3 tablespoons chopped fresh
    flat-leaf parsley

Heat half the butter and the marrow in a large heavy-based saucepan over low–medium heat. Add the onion and garlic, and sauté until softened. Add the rice and cook, stirring to coat, for 2 minutes, or until translucent.

Pour in the vermouth or white wine and saffron mixture and cook, stirring, until absorbed. Gradually add the stock, a ladle at a time, stirring constantly. Make sure all the liquid is absorbed before the next addition. Cook for 20–25 minutes, adding the stock gradually and stirring continuously, until the rice is al dente.

Stir in half the Parmesan cheese and the remaining butter. Season with salt and pepper. Serve topped with remaining Parmesan cheese and fresh parsley.

Rice with Peas
Risi e bisi

SERVES 4

2 pound 3 ounces fresh baby
    peas in their pods
1¾ quarts chicken stock,
    heated
6 tablespoons butter
1 tablespoon olive oil
1 medium onion, finely diced
1½ cups arborio or other
    risotto rice

½ cup grated Parmesan cheese
2 tablespoons finely chopped
    fresh flat-leaf parsley
1 tablespoon finely chopped
    fresh mint
salt and freshly ground black
    pepper

Shell the peas, reserving the pods, and place in a bowl.

Remove the strings from the pods and place pods in a medium saucepan. Pour in the stock and bring to a boil. Cook the pods until tender. Drain, reserving the liquid. Place the pods in a food processor or blender and blend until puréed.

Heat half the butter and the olive oil in a large, heavy-based saucepan over low–medium heat. Add the onion and sauté until softened. Add the peas and cook for 2 minutes. Add the rice, stirring to coat, and cook an additional 2 minutes, until translucent. >

Gradually add the stock, a ladle at a time, stirring constantly. Make sure almost all the liquid is absorbed before the next addition. Cook for 15 minutes, adding the stock gradually and stirring continuously. Add the purée and cook an additional 5–10 minutes, adding any remaining stock, until rice is al dente.

Stir in half the Parmesan cheese, the remaining butter and the parsley and mint. Season with salt and pepper. The mixture will be quite moist, a cross between a soup and a risotto. Serve topped with the remaining cheese.

Gorgonzola Risotto

SERVES 4

6 tablespoons butter
1 tablespoon olive oil
1 medium onion, finely diced
1 clove garlic, finely chopped
1½ cups arborio or other
   risotto rice
½ cup dry white wine

1 quart 10 fluid ounces chicken
   or vegetable stock, heated
7 ounces gorgonzola, cubed
½ cup chopped fresh flat-leaf
   parsley
salt and freshly ground black
   pepper

Heat half the butter and the olive oil in a large, heavy-based saucepan over low–medium heat. Add the onion and garlic, and sauté until softened. Add the rice, stirring to coat, and cook for 2 minutes, until translucent.

Pour in the wine and stir until absorbed. Gradually add the stock, a ladle at a time, stirring constantly. Make sure nearly all the liquid is absorbed before the next addition. Cook for 20 minutes, adding the stock gradually and stirring continuously.

Add the gorgonzola and cook an additional 3–5 minutes, adding any more stock if required, until the liquid has been absorbed and rice is al dente. Stir in the remaining butter and the parsley. Season with salt and pepper.

Wild Mushroom Risotto

1 tablespoon dried porcini
   mushrooms
2 cups warm water
3 cups chicken or vegetable
   stock
4 tablespoons olive oil
14 ounces mixed wild
   mushrooms, coarsely
   chopped
2 tablespoons finely chopped
   fresh oregano

6 tablespoons butter
1 medium onion, finely diced
2 cloves garlic, finely chopped
1½ cups arborio or other
   risotto rice
½ cup dry white wine
½ cup grated Parmesan cheese
salt and freshly ground black
   pepper

Soak the porcini mushrooms in the water for 30 minutes. Strain through a fine mesh sieve, reserving the liquid. Chop the mushrooms and set aside.

Pour the mushroom liquid and stock into a medium saucepan and bring to a simmer over medium heat. Decrease the heat to low to keep stock warm.

Heat 3 tablespoons of the olive oil in a large fry pan over medium–high heat. Add the wild mushrooms and oregano, and sauté until golden. Set aside.

Heat half the butter and the remaining olive oil in a large, heavy-based saucepan over low–medium heat. Add the onion, garlic and porcini mushrooms, and sauté until softened. Add the rice, stirring to coat, and cook for 2 minutes, until translucent.

Pour in the wine and cook, stirring, until absorbed. Gradually add the stock, a ladle at a time, stirring constantly. Make sure almost all the liquid is absorbed before the next addition. Cook for 15 minutes, adding the stock gradually and stirring continuously. Add the wild mushrooms and cook an additional 5–10 minutes, adding any more stock if required, until the liquid has been absorbed and rice is al dente.

Stir in half the Parmesan cheese and the remaining butter. Season with salt and pepper and serve topped with the remaining Parmesan cheese.

Squid Ink Risotto
Risotto nero

SERVES 4

SQUID

1¾ pounds squid with ink sacs

2 tablespoons olive oil

1 medium onion, finely diced

1 clove garlic, finely chopped

¾ cup dry white wine

juice of 1 lemon

2 tablespoons finely chopped
fresh flat-leaf parsley

salt and freshly ground black
pepper

RISOTTO

6 tablespoons butter

1 tablespoon olive oil

1½ cups arborio or other
risotto rice

¾ cup dry white wine

1 quart 10 fluid ounces fish
stock, heated

2 ink sacs (reserved from
squid)

salt and freshly ground black
pepper

To clean the squid, cut off the tentacles just below the ink sac. Remove the ink sacs, place in a small bowl and set aside. Remove and discard the guts, beak and cartilage from inside the body. Peel and discard the thin, colored membrane covering the squid and rinse under cold water. Slice the body into thin strips and the tentacles into short lengths. >

To cook the squid, heat the olive oil in a medium, heavy-based saucepan over low–medium heat. Add the onion and garlic, and sauté until softened. Pour in the wine and lemon juice and bring to a boil. Decrease the heat to low. Add the squid, cover, and cook, stirring occasionally, for 45–50 minutes, until tender. Stir in the parsley and season with salt and pepper.

To make the risotto, heat half the butter and the oil in a large, heavy-based saucepan over low–medium heat. Add the rice, stirring to coat, and cook for 2 minutes, until translucent. Pour in the wine and stir until absorbed. Gradually add the stock, a ladle at a time, stirring constantly. Make sure almost all the liquid is absorbed before the next addition. Cook for 15 minutes, adding the stock gradually and stirring continuously.

Add the ink, squeezing it from its sac, and cook an additional 5–10 minutes. Add more stock if required, until the liquid has been absorbed and rice is al dente. Stir in the remaining butter and season with salt and pepper. Serve risotto topped with the squid.

๛ Store-bought squid ink can be substituted for the sacs. For this recipe use the equivalent of two packets.

๛ You can ask your fish retailer to clean the squid for you.

Asparagus & Mint Risotto

SERVES 4

6 tablespoons butter
1 tablespoon olive oil
1 medium onion, finely diced
1 clove garlic, finely chopped
1½ cups arborio or other
   risotto rice
1⅔ quarts vegetable stock,
   heated

10½ ounces thin asparagus
   spears, trimmed and cut
   into 1-inch pieces
½ cup grated Parmesan cheese
3 tablespoons finely chopped
   fresh mint
salt and freshly ground black
   pepper

Heat half the butter and the olive oil in a large, heavy-based saucepan over low–medium heat. Add the onion and garlic, and sauté until softened. Add the rice, stirring to coat, and cook for 2 minutes, until translucent.

Gradually add the vegetable stock, a ladle at a time, stirring constantly. Make sure almost all the liquid is absorbed before the next addition. Continue cooking for 10 minutes. Add the asparagus and cook an additional 10–15 minutes, adding the vegetable stock gradually and stirring continuously, until the rice is al dente. Stir in the Parmesan cheese, mint and remaining butter. Season with salt and pepper.

Chicken & Spinach Risotto

SERVES 4

water, to blanch spinach
1 pound 5 ounces spinach
    leaves
6 tablespoons butter
1 tablespoon olive oil
1 medium onion, finely diced
2 cloves garlic, finely chopped
1½ cups arborio or other
    risotto rice

½ cup dry white wine
1 quart 10 fluid ounces
    chicken stock, heated
1 skinless chicken breast,
    thinly sliced
½ cup grated Pecorino cheese
salt and freshly ground black
    pepper

Place a large saucepan of water over high heat and bring to a boil. Blanch the spinach for 10 seconds, until wilted. Drain and squeeze out as much moisture as possible. Finely chop and set aside.

Heat half the butter and the olive oil in a large, heavy-based saucepan over low–medium heat. Add the onion and garlic, and sauté until softened. Add the rice, stirring to coat, and cook for 2 minutes, until translucent. Add the spinach and stir to combine.

Pour in the wine, stirring until it's absorbed. Gradually add the stock, a ladle at a time, stirring constantly. Make sure almost all the liquid is absorbed before the next addition. Cook for 15 minutes, then add the chicken. Cook an additional 5–10 minutes, adding any more stock if needed, until the liquid has been absorbed and rice is al dente.

Stir in half the Pecorino cheese and the remaining butter. Season with salt and pepper. Serve topped with the remaining cheese.

Seafood

Italy has an extensive coastline and seafood is an important part of the cuisine. Swordfish, mussels, clams, squid and tuna can all be found on Italian menus.

When purchasing fresh fish look for full and glossy eyes—if the eyes are sunken and dull, it isn't fresh. The gills should be red and the fish should smell fresh, not fishy. Ask your fish retailer to scale and gut the fish to save on time and mess at home. Non-traditional fish varieties have been used in some recipes here due to availability and in support of sustainable fishing practices.

When using shellfish, tap any opened ones gently on the counter top before cooking. If they do not close, discard.

< KING FISH WITH TAPENADE CRUST (PAGE 106)

King Fish with Tapenade Crust

SERVES 4

4 (6½-ounce) pieces king fish, or other firm white fish

TAPENADE CRUST
¾ cup pitted kalamata olives, coarsely chopped
¼ cup fresh flat-leaf parsley
1 clove garlic, coarsely chopped
½ tablespoon capers, rinsed
½ tablespoon finely chopped

fresh rosemary
2 anchovy fillets, coarsely chopped
2 teaspoons lemon juice
3 tablespoons extra-virgin olive oil
1½ cups fresh white breadcrumbs
salt and freshly ground black pepper

Preheat the oven to 400°F. Line a baking sheet with parchment (baking) paper.

To make the tapenade crust, place the olives, parsley, garlic, capers, rosemary and anchovies in a food processor or blender and pulse until coarsely blended. Add the lemon juice and gradually pour in the olive oil, blending to combine. Add the breadcrumbs, season with salt and pepper and stir to combine.

Place king fish on prepared baking sheet. Press a layer of crumb mixture on top of each fillet. Bake in the oven for 10 minutes, until crumbs are golden and fish is cooked through.

ॐ Substitutes for king fish include grouper, salmon and tuna. Firm white fish include mahi mahi, orange roughly and red snapper. Kalamata olives are large, deep purple Greek olives.

Sweet & Sour Tuna

SERVES 6

¹/₃ cup olive oil
2 medium onions, sliced
6 (6½-ounce) tuna steaks
½ cup red-wine vinegar
½ cup Marsala wine
1 tablespoon sugar
¾ cup pitted green olives

¼ cup raisins, plumped in
    a small bowl of water for
    20 minutes and drained
salt and freshly ground black
    pepper

Heat half the olive oil in a large fry pan over low–medium heat. Add the onions and sauté until softened. Transfer to a bowl and set aside.

Heat the remaining olive oil in the fry pan over medium heat. Cook the tuna steaks for 2 minutes on each side. Set aside with the onions. Pour the vinegar and Marsala wine into the pan. Add the sugar and bring to a boil, stirring to combine.

Decrease the heat to low and return the tuna and onions to the pan. Add the olives and raisins, and cook for 5–10 minutes, until sauce thickens slightly. Season with salt and pepper.

Seafood Stew
Cacciucco

SERVES 4

4 tablespoons olive oil

1 medium onion, finely chopped

3 cloves garlic, finely chopped

1 dried chili pepper, finely
chopped

¾ cup red wine

1 (1 pound 12-ounce) can diced
tomatoes

1 quart 10 fluid ounces fish stock

1 pound 7 ounces rockling, cut
into 2-inch chunks

1 pound 7 ounces John Dory,
cut into 2-inch chunks

1 pound 2 ounces black mussels,
cleaned and debearded

1 pound 2 ounces clams, cleaned

1 cup chopped fresh flat-leaf
parsley

salt and freshly ground black
pepper

Heat the olive oil in a large saucepan over low–medium heat. Add the onion, garlic and chili pepper, and sauté until softened. Pour in the wine and cook until reduced by half. Add the tomatoes and stock, and bring to a boil. Decrease the heat to low and simmer for 25–30 minutes, until slightly thickened and the flavors have developed.

Increase the heat to medium–high, add the fish, mussels and clams, cover and cook for 7–10 minutes, until mussels and clams have opened and fish is cooked through. (Discard any unopened shellfish.) Add the parsley, season with salt and pepper, and stir to combine.

☙ Substitutes for rockling include cod, dory, haddock and snapper. Substitutes for John Dory include halibut, sole and turbot.

Baked Snapper in Salt Crust

SERVES 4–6

4 pounds 6 ounces coarse sea
    salt
4 pounds 6 ounces whole
    snapper, scaled and cleaned
1 small bunch fresh thyme
salt and freshly ground black
    pepper
extra-virgin olive oil, to serve
juice of 1 lemon

Preheat the oven to 400°F. Spread a third of the sea salt over the bottom of a large baking sheet.

Stuff the cavity of the snapper with thyme and season with salt and pepper. Place fish on prepared baking sheet and cover completely with the remaining salt.

Bake in the oven for 45 minutes. Remove from the oven and allow to rest for 5 minutes. Crack open the salt crust and lift out the fish. Remove the skin and place fish on a serving plate. Drizzle with extra-virgin olive oil and lemon juice.

Ocean Trout with Salmoriglio

SERVES 4

4 (6½-ounce) ocean trout
    fillets, or other firm white
    fish fillets, pin boned

SALMORIGLIO
¼ cup extra-virgin olive oil
1 clove garlic, crushed
1 teaspoon finely grated lemon

    zest
2 tablespoons finely chopped
    fresh oregano
1 tablespoon finely chopped
    fresh flat-leaf parsley
3 tablespoons lemon juice
salt and freshly ground black
    pepper

Preheat the oven to 400°F. Lightly grease a large baking sheet.

To make the salmoriglio, place the extra-virgin olive oil, garlic, zest, oregano, parsley and lemon juice in a large bowl and whisk well to combine. Season with salt and pepper.

Place fish on the prepared baking sheet. Bake in the oven for 10 minutes, until fish is cooked through. Serve drizzled with salmoriglio.

☙ Salmoriglio is a Southern Italian condiment. It is usually served with fish and seafood, or grilled and roasted meats.

Rockling with Salsa Verde

SERVES 4

4 (6½-ounce) rockling fillets or other firm white fish fillets

SALSA VERDE
3 cups loosely packed fresh flat-leaf parsley
4 cornichons, coarsely chopped

1½ tablespoons capers, rinsed
1 clove garlic, coarsely chopped
3 anchovy fillets, coarsely chopped
1 tablespoon lemon juice
¼ cup extra-virgin olive oil
salt and freshly ground black pepper

Preheat the oven to 400°F. Line a baking sheet with a large sheet of aluminum foil.

To make the salsa verde, place the parsley, cornichons, capers, garlic and anchovies in a food processor or blender, and pulse until coarsely blended. Add the lemon juice and gradually pour in the extra-virgin olive oil, blending to combine. Season with salt and pepper. Transfer to a large bowl, add the fish and toss to coat.

Place fish on the prepared baking sheet, drizzle with any remaining salsa verde and fold foil over to cover fish. Bake in the oven for 10 minutes or until fish is cooked through.

ॐ Cornichons are tiny crisp, tart pickles.

Mussels with Tomatoes & Olives

SERVES 4

2 tablespoons olive oil

8 Roma tomatoes, diced

1/3 cup pitted kalamata olives

2 garlic cloves, crushed

4 sprigs dried oregano

2 bay leaves

3/4 cup dry white wine

juice of 1 lemon

4 pounds 6 ounces black
mussels, cleaned and
debearded

Heat the olive oil in a large, heavy-based saucepan over medium heat. Add the tomatoes, olives, garlic, oregano and bay leaves and cook for 2 minutes, until tomatoes begins to soften.

Increase the heat to high, pour in the wine and lemon juice, and bring to a boil. Add the mussels, cover, and cook for 7–10 minutes, until shells have opened. (Discard any unopened mussels.)

Whole Baked Baby Barramundi

SERVES 4

2 (2 pound 3 ounce) whole
   barramundi

ROSEMARY OIL
4 tablespoons olive oil
1 small red onion, thinly
   sliced
4 sprigs fresh rosemary, leaves
   picked
2 cloves garlic, thinly sliced
1 teaspoon finely grated lemon
   zest
salt and freshly ground black
   pepper

Preheat the oven to 400°F. Line two baking sheets large enough to hold the fish with aluminum foil.

To make the rosemary oil, combine olive oil, onion, rosemary, garlic and lemon zest together in a small bowl. Season with salt and pepper.

Score each fish twice in the thickest part near the head for even cooking. Coat the fish and inside the cavity with the rosemary oil. Place fish on the foil and wrap to enclose completely.

Bake in the oven for 20–30 minutes, until the fish is cooked through and flesh flakes easily.

༂ Barramundi are large-scaled river fish. Substitutes include halibut or sea bass.

Seafood Skewers
Spiedini di mare

SERVES 4

cold water, to soak bamboo
   skewers
1 pound 2 ounces swordfish,
   cut into 1-inch chunks
16 large raw (green) prawns,
   peeled and deveined
16 large scallops

MARINADE
$^{1}/_{3}$ cup olive oil
3 tablespoons lemon juice
3 tablespoons finely chopped
   fresh thyme
2 cloves garlic, crushed
salt and freshly ground black
   pepper

Soak eight large bamboo skewers in cold water for 1 hour, to prevent burning.
Alternatively use metal skewers.

For the marinade, combine the olive oil, lemon juice, thyme and garlic together
in a large bowl. Season with salt and pepper. Add the seafood, toss to coat,
cover with food wrap and refrigerate for 1 hour.

Preheat barbecue grill to high.

Thread two pieces of seafood onto each skewer. Cook for 2–3 minutes on
each side until cooked through.

꘎ Spiedini are Italian kebabs made with short skewers, or "little spits".

Roasted Rockling Wrapped in Pancetta

4 (6½-ounce) pieces rockling, or other firm white fish fillets

salt and freshly ground black pepper

8 thin slices pancetta

3 tablespoons olive oil

½ cup dry white wine

½ cup fish stock

4 stalks fresh parsley

4 sprigs fresh thyme

1 clove garlic, coarsely chopped

2 black peppercorns

1 bay leaf

Preheat the oven to 400°F.

Season the fish with salt and pepper. Wrap two slices of pancetta around each piece of fish and secure with a toothpick.

Heat the olive oil in a large fry pan over medium–high heat. Cook the fish for 2–3 minutes on each side, seam side down first, until golden-brown. Transfer to a small baking pan. Pour the wine into the fry pan and cook until reduced by half. Add the fish stock, parsley stalks, thyme sprigs, garlic, peppercorns and bay leaf, and bring to a boil. Pour the liquid into the baking pan with the fish and bake in the oven for 20 minutes, until fish is cooked through.

Mulloway with Caper & Anchovy Sauce

SERVES 4

4 (6½-ounce) pieces mulloway,
  or other firm white fish
1 tablespoon olive oil
salt and freshly ground black
  pepper

CAPER & ANCHOVY SAUCE
½ cup olive oil
8 anchovy fillets, finely
  chopped

3 tablespoons capers, finely
  chopped
1 tablespoon lemon juice
¼ cup finely chopped fresh
  flat-leaf parsley
salt and freshly ground black
  pepper

Preheat the oven to 400°F. Line a baking sheet with parchment (baking) paper.

To make the sauce, combine the olive oil, anchovies, capers and lemon juice in a small saucepan over low heat. Gently warm, stirring occasionally, until the anchovies dissolve. Stir in parsley and season with salt and pepper.

Place the fish on the prepared baking sheet, drizzle with olive oil and season with salt and pepper. Bake in the oven for 10 minutes or until fish is cooked through.

Serve drizzled with anchovy and caper sauce.

ॐ Mulloway is a large, saltwater fish. Substitutes include cod and grouper.

Baked Hapuka with Fennel & Orange

SERVES 4

4 small fennel bulbs with
  fronds attached
salted water, to blanch fennel
  bulbs
¼ cup kalamata olives
1 orange, segmented and zest
  finely grated

4 tablespoons olive oil
4 (6½-ounce) pieces hapuka,
  or other firm white fish
2 sprigs fresh rosemary
salt and freshly ground black
  pepper
½ cup dry white wine

Preheat the oven to 400°F.

Cut the fronds off the fennel and set aside. Trim and discard the tough outer layers. Bring a large pot of salted water to a boil. Blanch the fennel bulbs for 10 minutes, until tender. Drain and cut each bulb into quarters lengthwise.

Combine the fennel, olives, orange segments, zest and olive oil in a large bowl. Spoon half the fennel mixture over the bottom of a large baking dish. Place the fish, rosemary and reserved fennel fronds on top. Spoon over the remaining fennel mixture and season with salt and pepper.

Bake in the oven for 10 minutes. Add the wine and bake an additional 5 minutes, until fish is cooked through.

☙ Hapuka is a member of the grouper family, which can be used as a substitute.

Stuffed Squid

SERVES 4

4 medium squid, cleaned (see page 98) with tentacles retained
cold water, to rinse squid
1 cup breadcrumbs, made from day-old country-style bread
¼ cup chopped fresh flat-leaf parsley
4 tablespoons grated Parmesan cheese
2 tablespoons chopped kalamata olives
3 tablespoons olive oil
2 cloves garlic, crushed
salt and freshly ground pepper
1 small onion, finely chopped
¼ cup dry white wine
1 (1 pound 12-ounce) can diced tomatoes

Rinse the squid under cold water, pat dry with paper towels and set aside. Cut off the tentacles and discard the tough ends. Finely chop the remaining tentacles and set aside.

Place the tentacles, breadcrumbs, parsley, Parmesan cheese and olives in a medium bowl. Add one tablespoon of the olive oil and half the garlic and combine. Season with salt and pepper. Stuff the squid cavities with the breadcrumb mixture and secure the ends with toothpicks. Do not over-fill as the squid will shrink a little when cooked. >

Heat the remaining olive oil in a large fry pan over medium–high heat. Cook the squid for 1 minute on each side, until browned. Transfer to a plate and set aside.

Decrease the heat to low–medium. Add the onion and remaining garlic to the pan, and sauté until softened. Add the wine and cook until reduced by half. Add the tomatoes and bring to a boil. Decrease the heat to low and return the squid to the pan. Cover and cook for 30–35 minutes, until tender.

Lift the squid out of the pan using a slotted spoon. Discard the toothpicks, slice each squid into three and return to the pan to coat in sauce.

Parmesan Crumbed Flathead Tails

2 cups white breadcrumbs,
made from day-old country-
style bread

1/3 cup finely grated Parmesan
cheese

2 tablespoons finely chopped
fresh flat-leaf parsley

zest of 1 lemon

1/2 cup all-purpose flour

salt and freshly ground black
pepper

1 pound 9 ounces flathead
tails, boned and skinned

2 large eggs, lightly beaten

1 cup vegetable oil

1 lemon, cut into wedges

Combine the breadcrumbs, Parmesan cheese, parsley, and lemon zest in a shallow bowl. Place the flour in a shallow bowl and season with salt and pepper. Coat the flathead tails, dipping each one in flour, followed by egg and then the crumb mixture.

Preheat the vegetable oil in a large, heavy-based fry pan over medium heat. Fry the fish in batches, for 1 minute on each side, until golden. Transfer to a baking sheet lined with paper towels to drain.

Season with salt and serve with lemon wedges on the side.

Flathead have a flavor and texture similar to cod.

Meat & Poultry

Meat and poultry are served as the *secondo piatto* or 'second plate' in a traditional Italian meal.

Meats are often cooked slowly; braised and roasted for tenderness and flavor. In dishes such as osso bucco, braised lamb shanks, and braised rabbit, the meat is cooked with herb- and wine-infused stock until it is almost falling off the bone.

If you're short on time, try the veal saltimbocca or the scallopine with marsala sauce—they're quick and easy to prepare and sure to please.

< MEATBALLS (PAGE 128)

Meatballs

Polpette

SERVES 4

1 large egg, lightly beaten
2 tablespoons milk
1 cup fresh white breadcrumbs
¼ cup finely grated Parmesan
   cheese
1 tablespoon finely chopped
   fresh oregano
1 tablespoon finely chopped
   fresh parsley

3 anchovy fillets, finely
   chopped
1 clove garlic, finely chopped
salt and freshly ground black
   pepper
1 pound 2 ounces minced beef
¼ cup olive oil

Combine the egg, milk and breadcrumbs in a medium bowl and set aside to soak for 5 minutes. Then add the Parmesan cheese, oregano, parsley, anchovies and garlic. Season with salt and pepper. Add the minced beef and mix thoroughly. Shape tablespoonfuls into firm meatballs and place onto a tray.

Heat the olive oil in a large fry pan and fry the meatballs in batches for 3–4 minutes, turning, until browned all over and cooked through.

Serve with your choice of side dishes, or make a tomato sauce and serve with pasta.

↬ Minced beef is coarsely ground meat.

Veal Saltimbocca

SERVES 4

1¾ pounds veal scallopine
salt and freshly ground black
   pepper
8 slices prosciutto
8 fresh sage leaves

4 tablespoons butter
1 tablespoon olive oil
¼ cup all-purpose flour
1 cup dry white wine

Season the veal with salt and pepper. Lay a slice of prosciutto over each piece of veal, place a sage leaf on top and secure with a toothpick. Dust the veal lightly with flour.

Heat half the butter and olive oil in a large fry pan over high heat. Add half the veal to the pan and cook for 2 minutes on each side, prosciutto side first, until golden-brown. Transfer to a plate and remove the toothpicks. Repeat with remaining butter, olive oil and veal.

Pour in the white wine and boil until reduced by half. Return the veal to the pan and heat through.

  The name of this traditional Roman dish translates as 'to jump in the mouth'.

Veal Scallopine with Mushroom & Marsala Sauce

SERVES 4

1¾ pounds veal scallopine
¼ cup all-purpose flour
salt and freshly ground black
   pepper
4 tablespoons olive oil
1 tablespoon butter

½ small onion, finely diced
½ pound mushrooms, thinly
   sliced
½ cup Marsala wine
1 cup cream

Lay the scallopine between two double layers of food wrap and beat to an even thickness using a mallet. Season the flour with salt and pepper and coat the scallopine, dusting off excess.

In a large fry pan heat the olive oil over medium–high heat. Cook the veal in batches, for 2 minutes on each side, until golden-brown. Transfer to a plate and set aside.

Using the same pan heat the butter over low–medium heat. Add the onion and sauté until softened. Add the mushrooms and sauté an additional 5–10 minutes, until golden-brown. Pour in the Marsala wine and cook until reduced by half. Add the cream and bring to a boil. Reduce the heat to low and simmer gently until thickened slightly. Return veal to the pan. Toss to coat and warm through.

Osso Bucco

SERVES 4

¼ cup all-purpose flour
salt and freshly ground black
    pepper
4 (10½-ounce) center-cut veal
    shanks
4 tablespoons olive oil
3 tablespoons butter
2 stalks celery, finely diced
1 medium onion, finely diced
1 small carrot, finely diced
2 cloves garlic, finely chopped
¾ cup dry white wine
2 cups beef stock
4 sprigs fresh thyme

2 bay leaves

GREMOLATA
½ cup finely chopped fresh
    flat-leaf parsley
1 tablespoon finely grated
    lemon zest
1 clove garlic, crushed

Preheat the oven to 350°F.

Season the flour with salt and pepper and dust the veal. Place half the olive oil and the butter in a large flameproof casserole dish over medium–high heat. Cook the veal for 3–4 minutes, turning until browned all over. Transfer to a plate and set aside.

Heat the remaining olive oil in the dish. Add the celery, onion, carrot and garlic, and sauté until golden-brown. Pour in the wine and cook until reduced by half. Add the stock, thyme and bay leaves, and bring to a boil. Return the veal to the dish, cover and cook in the oven for 1½– 2 hours, until tender. The meat will almost be falling off the bones. Remove from the oven and skim off any excess fat.

To make the gremolata, combine the parsley, lemon zest and garlic in a small bowl.

Serve the osso bucco sprinkled with gremolata.

⇾ Serve with Risotto Milanese (page 91) to make the traditional northern Italian dish Osso Bucco Milanese—a hearty winter warmer.

Lamb with Artichokes

SERVES 4

12 small artichokes
cold water, to soak artichokes
juice of 1 lemon
¼ cup all-purpose flour
salt and freshly ground black
 pepper
8–12 lamb cutlets
¼ cup olive oil
1 small onion, sliced
2 cloves garlic, finely chopped

3½ ounces pancetta, finely
 chopped
2 bay leaves
1 tablespoon finely chopped
 fresh oregano
1 tablespoon finely chopped
 fresh thyme
1 cup dry white wine
1 cup chicken stock
1 cup passata

Peel the stems of the artichokes and remove the dark, tough outer leaves, exposing the light tender ones. Trim the tops and scoop out the chokes. Cut artichokes into quarters.

Fill a bowl large enough to hold the artichokes with cold water and add the lemon juice. Place artichokes in the lemon water and let soak for 10 minutes or until required.

Season the flour with salt and pepper and dust the lamb. Heat 2 tablespoons of the olive oil in a large flameproof casserole dish or heavy-based saucepan over medium–high heat. Add half of the lamb and cook for 2 minutes on each side, until browned. Transfer to a plate and set aside. >

Repeat with another 2 tablespoons of olive oil and the remaining lamb.

Heat the remaining oil over low–medium heat and sauté the onion and garlic until softened. Add the pancetta and herbs, and cook an additional 5–10 minutes, until golden-brown. Pour in the wine and cook until reduced by half. Pour in the stock and passata, and bring to a boil. Decrease the heat to low, add the drained artichokes, cover and cook for 10 minutes. Return the lamb to the dish and cook an additional 15 minutes.

Veal with Tuna Sauce

Vitello tonnato

SERVES 6

TUNA SAUCE

2 large egg yolks

1 tablespoon Dijon mustard

2 tablespoons lemon juice

¾ cup olive oil

1 (6½-ounce) can tuna in oil, drained

2 tablespoons capers, rinsed

4 anchovy fillets, finely chopped

salt and freshly ground pepper

VEAL

1¾ pounds veal topside (round steak)

water, to cover veal

1 onion, roughly chopped

1 small carrot, chopped

1 stalk celery, roughly chopped

3 fresh parsley stalks

2 bay leaves

2 black peppercorns

1 tablespoon white-wine vinegar

½ tablespoon salt

To prepare the tuna sauce, blend egg yolks, mustard and lemon juice in a food processor or blender. Gradually add olive oil in a thin stream, until thickened. Add the tuna, capers and anchovies, and blend to a smooth sauce. Add a little warm water if the sauce is too thick. Season with salt and pepper.

Put all ingredients for the veal in a large, heavy-based saucepan. Add enough water to cover the veal, stir, and bring to a simmer over medium–high heat. Decrease the heat to low, cover and cook for 2–2½ hours, until tender. Leave veal in the stock to cool, then remove from liquid and slice thinly. Spoon the sauce over.

Chicken Cacciatore

SERVES 4

4 tablespoons olive oil

1 tablespoon butter

3½ pounds whole chicken, cut into 8 pieces

salt and freshly ground black pepper

1 large onion, sliced

1 stalk celery, finely diced

2 cloves garlic, finely chopped

½ cup dry white wine

½ cup chicken stock

1 (1 pound 12-ounce) can diced tomatoes

2 bay leaves

1 tablespoon chopped fresh oregano

Heat half the olive oil and the butter in a large, heavy-based fry pan over medium–high heat. Season the chicken with salt and pepper, and cook in batches, for 8–10 minutes, turning occasionally until browned all over. Transfer to a plate and set aside.

Add the remaining olive oil to the pan and decrease the heat to low–medium. Add the onion, celery and garlic, and sauté until softened. Pour in the wine and cook until reduced by half. Add the stock, tomatoes, bay leaves and oregano, and bring to a boil. Decrease the heat to low and return the chicken to the pan. Cover and cook for 35–40 minutes, until the chicken is cooked and the sauce has thickened.

Braised Rabbit with Fennel, Olives & Rosemary

SERVES 6

⅓ cup olive oil
¼ cup all-purpose flour
salt and freshly ground pepper
2 rabbits, jointed by butcher
3 tablespoons butter
1 large onion, sliced
1 clove garlic, finely chopped
5 ounces pancetta, diced
2 fennel bulbs, trimmed and
   quartered lengthways

1 cup dry white wine
3 cups chicken stock
½ cup small black olives
sprig of rosemary
2 bay leaves
½ tablespoon finely grated
   orange zest

Preheat the oven to 350°F.

Heat the olive oil in a heavy-based fry pan over medium–high heat. Season flour with salt and pepper. Dust the rabbits with flour and cook in batches for 3–4 minutes, until browned. Transfer to a large casserole dish.

Heat butter in the pan over low–medium heat. Add onion and garlic, and sauté until softened. Add the pancetta and fennel, and sauté until golden. Pour in the white wine and cook until reduced by half. Add chicken stock, olives, rosemary, bay leaves and orange zest, and bring to a boil. Pour stock over the rabbits, cover and cook in the oven for 1–1½ hours, until tender.

Pancetta Roasted Chicken

SERVES 4

3½ pound whole chicken
cold water, to rinse chicken
1 small lemon, halved
4 tablespoons olive oil
1 tablespoon chopped fresh
   sage

1 tablespoon chopped fresh
   rosemary
salt and ground black pepper
6 thin slices pancetta
½ cup dry white wine
3 tablespoons water

Preheat the oven to 350°F.

Rinse the chicken under cold running water and pat dry with paper towels. Put the lemon halves inside the cavity and truss the legs together using kitchen string. Place the chicken, breast side up, in a roasting pan.

Combine the olive oil, sage and rosemary in a small bowl and season with salt and pepper. Rub the herb mixture over the chicken and wrap with pancetta, tucking the ends underneath the chicken. Pour the white wine into the pan.

Cook in the oven for 1½ hours, basting occasionally, until golden-brown and juices run clear when thigh is pierced. Transfer to a serving platter, cover with foil and set aside for 10 minutes. Place the roasting pan over medium heat. Add the water to the pan juices and heat, stirring to combine. Pour juices over the chicken and serve.

Rolled Roast Pork
Porchetta

SERVES 6–8

4 pounds 6 ounces pork loin, boned and skinned, skin reserved

4 tablespoons olive oil

3 teaspoons salt

4 tablespoons finely chopped fresh rosemary

2 tablespoons finely chopped fresh sage

2 teaspoons fennel seeds

2 cloves garlic, crushed

freshly ground black pepper

½ cup water

⅓ cup dry white wine

Preheat the oven to 325°F.

Score the pork skin in a crisscross pattern using a shape knife. Rub 1 tablespoon olive oil into the skin and sprinkle with 2 teaspoons of the salt. Set aside.

Combine 2 tablespoons of the olive oil, the remaining salt, the rosemary, sage, fennel seeds and garlic in a small bowl and season with pepper.

Lay the pork loin on a clean counter top, trim and discard any excess fat. Turn over and spread the herb mixture over the flesh. Roll up the pork and wrap the skin around the outside. Secure firmly with kitchen string and place in a roasting pan. Pour in the water and white wine, and cook in the oven for 2 hours, basting occasionally with the pan juices. ❯

Increase the oven temperature to 350°F.

Cook the pork an additional hour. Remove from the oven, cover with aluminum foil and set aside to rest for 10 minutes. Remove string and slice the pork into ¾-inch thick slices. Serve drizzled with pan juices.

Chicken Scarpariello

SERVES 4

¼ cup all-purpose flour
salt and freshly ground black
    pepper
8 chicken thighs
4 tablespoons olive oil
4 tablespoons butter

1 small onion, finely chopped
2 cloves garlic, finely chopped
juice of 2 lemons
1 cup chicken stock
2 tablespoons chopped
    oregano

Preheat the oven to 350°F.

Season the flour with salt and pepper. Dust the chicken with flour.

Heat the olive oil in a large fry pan over medium–high heat. Cook the chicken thighs for 2–3 minutes on each side, until browned all over. Transfer to a baking sheet and cook in the oven for 20–25 minutes, until cooked through.

Melt the butter in a medium fry pan over low–medium heat. Add the onion and garlic, and sauté until softened. Add the lemon juice and chicken stock and simmer until reduced by half. Stir in the oregano.

Serve the chicken drizzled with sauce.

Veal Sorrentino

SERVES 4

1 cup breadcrumbs, made
   from day-old country-style
   bread
2 tablespoons finely chopped
   fresh basil
2 tablespoons grated Parmesan
   cheese
¼ cup all-purpose flour
salt and freshly ground black
   pepper

1 eggplant, cut lengthwise into
   8 slices
2 eggs, lightly beaten
½ cup olive oil
1¾ pounds veal scallopine
1¼ cups passata
8 thin slices prosciutto
8 slices mozzarella
¼ cup dry white wine
½ cup chicken stock

Preheat the oven to 350°F.

Combine the breadcrumbs, basil and Parmesan cheese together in a medium bowl. Place the flour in a small bowl and season with salt and pepper. Pour eggs into a shallow bowl. Coat the eggplant, dipping the slices into the flour, followed by eggs and then the crumb mixture.

Heat half of the olive oil in a large fry pan over medium–high heat. Cook the eggplant for 1 minute on each side, until golden-brown. Set aside. >

Heat the remaining olive oil in the pan. Season the veal with salt and pepper, and cook for 1 minute on each side until browned. Arrange the veal in a large baking dish. Top each piece with a slice of prosciutto followed by a spoonful of passata, a folded piece of eggplant and a slice of mozzarella.

Pour the white wine and chicken stock into the fry pan, bring to a boil and pour into the baking dish with the veal. Bake in the oven for 5 minutes, until the cheese has melted.

Serve drizzled with pan juices.

Braised Lamb Shanks
with White Beans

SERVES 4

¼ cup all-purpose flour
salt and freshly ground pepper
4 lamb shanks
4 tablespoons olive oil
3 tablespoons butter
2 stalks celery, finely diced
1 medium onion, finely diced
1 small carrot, finely diced
2 cloves garlic, finely chopped

1 cup red wine
1 (14½-ounce) can diced
    tomatoes
2 cups chicken stock
2 bay leaves
14 ounces dried cannellini
    (white Italian kidney) beans,
    rinsed
¼ cup fresh flat-leaf parsley

Preheat the oven to 350°F.

Season the flour with salt and pepper. Dust the lamb with flour. Heat half the olive oil and the butter in a large casserole dish over medium–high heat. Cook the lamb shanks for 3–4 minutes, turning, until browned. Transfer to a plate.

Heat the remaining olive oil in the dish, add celery, onion, carrot and garlic, and sauté until golden-brown. Pour in the red wine and cook until reduced by half. Add the tomatoes, chicken stock and bay leaves and bring to a boil.

Return lamb to the dish, cover, and cook in the oven for 1 hour. Add the cannellini beans and cook for 30–45 minutes, until tender. Stir in the parsley.

Beef Involtini

SERVES 4

½ cup olive oil
1 onion, finely chopped
2 cloves garlic, crushed
½ cup red wine
2 (14-ounce) cans crushed
   tomatoes
1 tablespoon tomato paste
1 teaspoon sugar
4 thick (1-inch) slices beef fillet

¼ cup sun-dried tomatoes,
   finely chopped
¼ cup pine nuts, lightly
   toasted and finely chopped
¼ cup grated Pecorino cheese
salt and freshly ground black
   pepper
4 slices prosciutto, halved
16 fresh basil leaves

Heat 2 tablespoons of the olive oil in a medium saucepan over low–medium heat. Add the onion and garlic, and sauté until softened. Pour in the red wine and cook until reduced by half. Add the tomatoes, tomato paste and sugar, and bring to a boil. Reduce the heat and gently simmer for 20 minutes. Season with salt and pepper. Pass the sauce through a fine mesh sieve and return to the pan. Keep warm.

Butterfly the beef fillets and lay them between two double layers of food wrap. Beat the fillets to half their thickness using a mallet, then cut in half widthwise.

Combine the sun-dried tomatoes, pine nuts and Pecorino cheese in a medium bowl and season with salt and pepper.

Lay half a slice of prosciutto on each piece of beef and place two basil leaves on top. Sprinkle with the sun-dried tomato mixture. Roll up the beef to enclose the filling and secure with a toothpick.

Heat 2 tablespoons of the olive oil in a large, heavy-based fry pan over medium–high heat. Add half the involtini to the pan and cook for 3–4 minutes, turning, until well-browned. Transfer to a plate. Repeat with the remaining olive oil and involtini. Return all the rolls to the pan and pour in the sauce. Gently simmer for 25–30 minutes.

Involtini, or "little bundles", are Italian beef roulades, also called braciole.

Pizza

Pizza as we know it today is thought to have evolved in Naples in the early 1800s. It was here the Margherita was later named in honor of the Queen of Italy.

In Italy, pizza crusts are crisp and thin, and toppings include fresh herbs, mozzarella cheese, cured meats and rich tomato sauce.

To achieve the best results, proof pizza dough in a warm place in the kitchen without any cold drafts. Cold air inhibits the development of the yeast and affects the lightness of the dough.

Pizza stones, available at most kitchenware stores, create a more authentic crisp pizza crust. Preheat the stone in a hot oven for at least 30 minutes. Shape the pizza dough, place on top of the stone, scatter toppings, and bake in the oven until crisp.

‹ PIZZA DOUGH (PAGE 156)

Pizza Dough

MAKES 4 (10-INCH) PIZZAS

1 tablespoon dry yeast
1 cup lukewarm water
2²/₃ cups all-purpose flour
pinch of salt
1 tablespoon olive oil

Combine the yeast and water in a small bowl. Place the flour and salt in a large bowl, and make a well in the center. Pour the yeast mixture and oil into the well and use a fork to gradually combine the flour with the liquid. Turn the dough out onto a clean kitchen surface and knead for 10–15 minutes, until a smooth elastic ball is formed.

Place the dough in a large, lightly greased bowl. Cover with a clean kitchen towel and put in a warm place to proof for 1½–2 hours, until doubled in size. Turn the dough out onto the kitchen surface and punch out all the air out. Divide the dough into quarters and place on a lightly oiled baking sheet. Cover with a kitchen towel and put in a warm place for 20–30 minutes, until doubled in size. Dough is now ready to use.

Capricciosa

MAKES 4 (10-INCH) PIZZAS

olive oil, to prepare pizza pans
1 quantity pizza dough
  (page 156)

TOPPINGS
6½ ounces portobello
  mushrooms, thinly sliced
8 thin slices prosciutto

6½ ounces cherry tomatoes
4 marinated artichoke hearts,
  sliced
¼ cup pitted black olives
10½ ounces buffalo
  mozzarella, torn
extra-virgin olive oil

Preheat the oven to 425°F. Heat two 10-inch metal pizza pans in the oven for 30 minutes.

Remove pizza pans from oven and brush with olive oil. Stretch and shape two portions of the dough to fit the oiled pizza pans. Allow to rest for a few minutes.

Arrange half of the topping ingredients on top of each of the pizza dough. Drizzle with extra-virgin olive oil. Cook pizzas for 10–12 minutes, until golden-brown. Remove pizzas from the pans and bake on the oven rack an additional 5 minutes, until bottoms are crisp. Slice and serve.

Four Seasons

Quattro stagioni

MAKES 4 (10-INCH) PIZZAS

1 quantity pizza dough
(page 156)

TOPPINGS
1 cup passata
10½ ounces buffalo mozzarella
cheese, sliced

6½ ounces button mushrooms,
thinly sliced
⅔ cup pitted black olives
8 marinated artichoke hearts,
sliced
8 thin slices prosciutto
extra-virgin olive oil

Preheat the oven to 425°F. Heat two 10-inch metal pizza pans in the oven for
30 minutes.

Remove pizza pans from oven and brush with olive oil. Stretch and shape two
portions of the dough to fit the oiled pizza pans. Allow to rest for a few minutes.

Spread half of the passata onto each of the pizza dough and scatter each pizza
with half of the mozzarella. Arrange a quarter of each topping over each pizza:
one quarter with mushroom, one with olives, one artichoke and the remaining
one prosciutto. Drizzle with olive oil and cook for 10–12 minutes, until golden-
brown. Remove the pizzas from the pans and bake on the oven rack an
additional 5 minutes, until bottoms are crisp. Slice and serve.

Spicy Salami

MAKES 4 (10-INCH) PIZZAS

1 quantity pizza dough
  (page 156)

TOPPINGS
1 cup passata
5 ounces thinly sliced spicy
  salami, such as pepperoni
  or soppressata

¼ teaspoon chili flakes
10½ ounces buffalo
  mozzarella, torn
extra-virgin olive oil

Preheat the oven to 420°F. Heat two 10-inch metal pizza pans in the oven for 30 minutes.

Remove pizza pans from the oven and brush with olive oil. Stretch and shape two portions of the dough to fit the pizza pans. Allow to rest for a few minutes.

Spread half of the passata onto each of the pizza dough. Scatter each pizza with half of the toppings and drizzle with olive oil. Bake for 10–12 minutes, until golden-brown. Remove the pizzas from the pans and bake on the oven rack an additional 5 minutes, until bottoms are crisp. Slice and serve.

Potato & Rosemary

MAKES 4 (10-INCH) PIZZAS

1 quantity pizza dough
(page 156)

TOPPINGS
4 medium potatoes, thinly
sliced
10½ ounces fontina cheese,
thinly sliced

1 cup shaved Pecorino cheese
4 tablespoons fresh rosemary
leaves
salt and freshly ground black
pepper
extra-virgin olive oil

Preheat the oven to 425°F. Heat two 10-inch metal pizza pans in the oven for 30 minutes.

Remove pizza pans from oven and brush with olive oil. Stretch and shape two portions of the dough to fit pizza pans. Allow to rest for a few minutes.

Arrange half the potato slices over each of the pizza dough. Sprinkle each pizza with half of the cheese and the rosemary. Season with salt and pepper and drizzle with olive oil. Bake for 10–12 minutes, until golden-brown. Remove the pizzas from the pans and bake on the oven rack an additional 5 minutes, until bottoms are crisp. Slice and serve.

Romana

1 quantity pizza dough
(page 156)

TOMATO SAUCE
2 tablespoons olive oil
1 small onion, sliced
2 cloves garlic, finely chopped
1 (14-ounces) can whole peeled
tomatoes, coarsely chopped
2 tablespoons finely chopped
oregano

½ teaspoon sugar
salt and freshly ground black
pepper

TOPPINGS
14 ounces buffalo mozzarella,
sliced
8 anchovy fillets
3 tablespoons chopped fresh
oregano
extra-virgin olive oil

Preheat the oven to 425°F. Heat two 10-inch metal pizza pans in the oven for 30 minutes.

To make the sauce, heat the olive oil in a saucepan over medium heat. Add the onion and garlic, and sauté until softened. Add the tomatoes, oregano and sugar and bring to a boil. Decrease the heat to low–medium and gently simmer for 10–12 minutes, until thickened and flavors have developed. Season with salt and pepper, and set aside. >

Remove pizza pans from oven and brush with olive oil. Stretch and shape two portions of the dough to fit oiled pizza pans. Allow to rest for a few minutes.

Spread half of the sauce over each of the pizza dough. Arrange half the mozzarella slices over each of the tops. Scatter each pizza with half the oregano and anchovies. Drizzle each pizza with olive oil. Bake for 10–12 minutes, until golden-brown. Remove the pizzas from the pans and bake on the oven rack an additional 5 minutes, until bottoms are crisp. Slice and serve.

Four Cheeses
Quattro formaggi

MAKES 4 (10-INCH) PIZZAS

1 quantity pizza dough
  (page 156)

TOPPINGS
7 ounces fontina cheese,
  grated
6½ ounces Asiago cheese,
  grated

5 ounces buffalo mozzarella,
  thinly sliced
4½ ounces gorgonzola,
  crumbled
16 pitted black olives
extra-virgin olive oil

Preheat the oven to 425°F. Heat two 10-inch metal pizza pans in the oven for 30 minutes.

Remove pans from oven and brush with olive oil. Stretch and shape two portions of the dough to fit metal pizza pans. Allow to rest for a few minutes.

Scatter half of each cheese over each of the pizza dough. Place four olives on each pizza and drizzle with olive oil. Bake pizzas for 10–12 minutes, until golden-brown. Remove the pizzas from the pans and bake on the oven rack an additional 5 minutes, until bottoms are crisp. Slice and serve.

Vegetarian

1 quantity pizza dough
  (page 156)

TOPPINGS
1 cup passata
1 medium zucchini, thinly
  sliced and grilled
1 small eggplant, thinly sliced
  and grilled
2 roasted red bell peppers,
  sliced

¼ cup pitted black olives
4 tablespoons chopped fresh
  oregano
5 ounces buffalo mozzarella,
  torn
5 ounces soft goat cheese,
  crumbled
extra-virgin olive oil

Preheat the oven to 425°F. Heat two 10-inch metal pizza pans in the oven for 30 minutes.

Remove pizza pans from oven and brush with olive oil. Stretch and shape two portions of the dough to fit pizza pans. Allow to rest for a few minutes.

Spread half of the passata onto each of the pizza dough. Arrange the topping ingredients over the passata. Drizzle with olive oil and bake for 10–12 minutes, until golden-brown. Remove the pizzas from the pans and bake on the oven rack for an additional 5 minutes, until bottoms are crisp. Slice and serve.

Margherita

MAKES 4 (10-INCH) PIZZAS

1 quantity pizza dough
(page 156)

TOMATO SAUCE
2 tablespoons olive oil
1 small onion, sliced
2 cloves garlic, finely chopped
1 (14-ounce) can whole peeled
tomatoes, coarsely chopped
2 tablespoons finely chopped
fresh oregano

½ teaspoon sugar
salt and freshly ground black
pepper

TOPPINGS
14 ounces buffalo mozzarella,
sliced
½ cup fresh basil leaves, torn
extra-virgin olive oil

Preheat the oven to 425°F. Heat two 10-inch metal pizza pans in the oven for 30 minutes.

To make the sauce, heat the olive oil in a saucepan over medium heat. Add the onion and garlic, and sauté until softened. Add the tomatoes, oregano and sugar, and bring to a boil. Decrease the heat to low–medium and gently simmer for 10–12 minutes, until thickened and flavors have developed. Season with salt and pepper, and set aside.

Remove pizza pans from oven and brush with olive oil. Stretch and shape two portions of the dough to fit pizza pans. Allow to rest for a few minutes.

Spread half of the sauce over each of the pizza dough. Arrange half of the mozzarella slices over each of the tops. Scatter each pizza with half of the basil and drizzle with olive oil. Bake for 10–12 minutes, until golden-brown. Remove the pizzas from the pans and bake on the oven rack an additional 5 minutes, until bases are crisp. Slice and serve.

ᐎ Margherita pizza is considered the most basic pizza with simple ingredients.

White
Bianco

MAKES 4 (10-INCH) PIZZAS

1 quantity pizza dough
(page 156)

TOPPINGS
10 ounces mascarpone cheese
5 ounces soft goat cheese,
sliced

½ teaspoon chili pepper flakes
salt and freshly ground black
pepper
3 ounces arugula leaves
extra-virgin olive oil

Preheat the oven to 425°F. Heat two 10-inch metal pizza pans in the oven for 30 minutes.

Remove pizza pans from oven and brush with olive oil. Stretch and shape two portions of the dough to fit pizza pans. Allow to rest for a few minutes.

Using half of each topping, spread each of the pizza dough with mascarpone and dot with slices of goat cheese. Sprinkle with chili pepper flakes and season with salt and pepper. Bake for 10–12 minutes, until golden-brown. Remove the pizzas from the pans and bake on the oven rack an additional 5 minutes, until bottoms are crisp. Top each pizza with half of the arugula and drizzle with olive oil. Slice and serve.

↷ Bianco pizza is often made with béchamel sauce.

Prosciutto & Egg

MAKES 4 (10-INCH) PIZZAS

1 quantity pizza dough
(page 156)

TOPPING
12 thin slices prosciutto
10 ounces buffalo mozzarella,
torn

4 ounces cherry tomatoes
8 fresh basil leaves, torn
extra-virgin olive oil
4 large eggs
salt and freshly ground black
pepper

Preheat the oven to 425°F. Heat two 10-inch metal pizza pans in the oven for 30 minutes.

Remove pizza pans from oven and brush with olive oil. Stretch and shape two portions of the dough to fit pizza pans. Allow to rest for a few minutes.

Arrange half of the prosciutto, mozzarella and tomatoes over each of the pizza dough. Scatter each pizza with half of the basil and drizzle with olive oil. Bake for 10–12 minutes, until golden-brown. Remove the pizzas from the pans, crack an egg in the center of each pizza and season with salt and pepper. Bake on the oven rack an additional 5 minutes, until eggs are just cooked and bottoms are crisp. Slice and serve.

Spicy Eggplant Calzone

MAKES 4

1 quantity pizza dough
  (page 156)

FILLING
4 tablespoons extra-virgin
  olive oil
2 medium eggplants, cut into
  ¾-inch cubes
1 clove garlic, finely chopped
1 teaspoon chili pepper flakes

1 cup passata
½ cup pitted kalamata olives,
  coarsely chopped
4 tablespoons chopped fresh
  flat-leaf parsley
salt and freshly ground black
  pepper
7 ounces buffalo mozzarella,
  sliced

Heat the olive oil in a medium saucepan over medium heat. Add the eggplant, garlic and chili pepper flakes, and sauté for 5–10 minutes, until golden-brown. Add the passata and olives, and cook an additional 5 minutes. Remove from the heat, stir in the parsley and season with salt and pepper. Transfer to a bowl and refrigerate until cold.

Preheat the oven to 425°F. Heat two 10-inch metal pizza pans in the oven for 30 minutes.

Remove pizza pans from oven and brush with olive oil. Stretch and shape two portions of the dough to fit pizza pans. Allow to rest for a few minutes.

Spoon a quarter of the spiced eggplant mixture onto one half of the bottom of one calzone. Sprinkle with a quarter of the mozzarella. Fold the dough over to encase the filling, pinching the edges to seal. Repeat with the second calzone. Brush calzones with olive oil and bake for 15 minutes, until crisp and lightly golden.

Repeat the process with any remaining dough and filling.

A calzone is an Italian turnover shaped like a crescent, and filled with pizza ingredients.

Bolognese Calzone

MAKES 4

1 quantity pizza dough
(page 156)

FILLING
2 tablespoons extra-virgin
olive oil
½ small onion, diced
2 cloves garlic, finely chopped
1 pound 2 ounces minced beef

1½ cups passata
1 tablespoon tomato paste
2 tablespoons finely chopped
fresh oregano
salt and freshly ground black
pepper
3½ ounces buffalo mozzarella,
sliced

Heat the olive oil in a medium saucepan over low–medium heat. Add the onion and garlic, and sauté until softened. Add the minced beef and cook, stirring to break up, for 5 minutes, until browned. Add the passata, tomato paste and oregano, and gently simmer for 45–60 minutes, until thick and flavors have developed. Season with salt and pepper, and set aside to cool.

Preheat the oven to 425°F. Heat two 10-inch metal pizza pans in the oven for 30 minutes.

Remove pizza pans from oven and brush with olive oil. Stretch and shape two portions of the dough to fit pizza pans. Allow to rest for a few minutes. **>**

Spread a quarter of the bolognese sauce over half of the bottom of one calzone and sprinkle with a quarter of the mozzarella. Fold the dough over to encase the filling, pinching the edges to seal. Repeat with the second calzone. Brush calzones with olive oil and bake for 15 minutes, until crisp and golden.

Repeat the process with any remaining dough and filling.

∽ Calzones are ideal for using up leftover bolognese sauce. If making fresh, the sauce can be made the night before to allow the flavors to develop and to save preparation time on the day.

Mushroom & Roasted Bell Pepper Calzone

MAKES 4

1 quantity pizza dough
(page 156)

FILLING
2 tablespoons extra-virgin olive
oil
9 ounces button mushrooms,
thinly sliced

2 cloves garlic, finely chopped
9 ounces chargrilled bell
peppers, thinly sliced
4 tablespoons chopped basil
salt and ground black pepper
9 ounces ricotta cheese,
crumbled

Heat the olive oil in a saucepan over low–medium heat. Add mushrooms and garlic, and sauté until golden. Remove from heat and stir in the bell peppers and basil. Season with salt and pepper. Refrigerate until cold.

Preheat the oven to 425°F. Heat two 10-inch metal pizza pans in the oven for 30 minutes.

Remove pizza pans from oven and brush with olive oil. Stretch and shape two portions of the dough to fit pizza pans. Allow to rest for a few minutes.

Spoon a quarter of the mushroom mixture over half of the bottom of one calzone. Sprinkle with a quarter of the ricotta. Fold the dough over to encase the filling, pinching the edges to seal. Repeat with the second calzone. Brush calzones with olive oil and bake for 15 minutes, until crisp and golden.

Repeat the process with any remaining dough and filling.

Cheesy Soppressa
& Tomato Calzone

MAKES 4

1 quantity pizza dough
(page 156)
extra-virgin olive oil, for
brushing

FILLING
1 cup passata
7 ounces fontina cheese,
thickly sliced

7 ounces buffalo mozzarella,
thickly sliced
12 slices hot soppressa (Italian
pork salami), coarsely
chopped
12 cherry tomatoes, halved
12 basil leaves
salt and freshly ground black
pepper

Preheat the oven to 425°F. Heat two 10-inch metal pizza pans in the oven for 30 minutes.

Remove pizza pans from oven and brush with olive oil. Stretch and shape two portions of the dough to fit pizza pans. Allow to rest for a few minutes.

Spread half of the passata over the bottoms of the calzones. Arrange a quarter of the filling ingredients over half of one of the calzones and season with salt and pepper. Fold the dough over to encase the filling, pinching the edges to seal. Repeat with the second calzone. Brush calzones with olive oil and bake for 15 minutes, or until crisp and golden.

Repeat the process with any remaining dough and filling ingredients.

Sides & Extras

A side dish of vegetables or salad, known as the *contorno*, always accompanies the second course of fish, meat or poultry. Vegetable dishes are braised, grilled, marinated and roasted, while salads are crisp and dressed with vinegar. All are flavored with fresh herbs and drizzled with extra-virgin olive oil.

Try serving the arugula and Parmesan cheese salad alongside roasted rockling. Or roasted tomatoes and grilled zucchini with a chicken dish. For an alfresco lunch or equally satisfying evening meal serve a selection of sides (perhaps all vegetarian) with some fresh focaccia.

Extras such as tapenade, pesto and salsa verde can be made days in advance and stored in the refrigerator. Toss with some al dente pasta for a simple quick meal, or use to marinate fish, meat or poultry and then grill or bake in the oven.

❮ PEAR, RADICCHIO & WALNUT SALAD (PAGE 184)

Pear, Radicchio & Walnut Salad

SERVES 4

3 tablespoons extra-virgin
   olive oil
2 tablespoons lemon juice
salt and freshly ground black
   pepper
4 heads radicchio (red-leafed
   Italian chicory)
2 pears, quartered, cored and
   thinly sliced
1/3 cup walnut halves, lightly
   toasted

Whisk the olive oil and lemon juice together in a small bowl. Season with salt and pepper.

Remove and discard the outer leaves of the radicchio. Roughly tear the remaining leaves and place in a medium bowl. Add the pear and walnuts. Pour the dressing over and toss to coat.

Arugula & Parmesan Salad

SERVES 4

2 tablespoons extra-virgin
    olive oil
2 tablespoons balsamic vinegar
1 teaspoon Dijon mustard
pinch of sugar
salt and freshly ground black
    pepper
4½ ounces arugula leaves
¾ cup shaved Parmesan cheese

Whisk the olive oil, vinegar, mustard and sugar together in a small bowl. Season with salt and pepper.

Put the arugula in a medium bowl. Pour the dressing over and toss to coat. Place in a serving bowl and sprinkle with Parmesan cheese.

Fennel, Orange & Hazelnut Salad

SERVES 4

3 oranges
2 medium fennel bulbs,
  trimmed
¼ cup hazelnuts, lightly
  toasted and coarsely
  chopped
2 tablespoons extra-virgin
  olive oil
freshly ground black pepper

Peel the oranges and cut off the pith. Slice oranges into thin rounds, removing any seeds.

Thinly slice the fennel and place in a medium bowl. Add the orange slices and hazelnuts. Drizzle with olive oil and toss to coat.

Season with freshly ground pepper.

Tomato & Cucumber Bread Salad
Panzanella

SERVES 4

9 ounce stale country-style
   bread
4 tablespoons cold water
4 medium vine-ripened
   tomatoes, diced
2 small cucumbers, peeled and
   diced
1 small red onion, finely sliced
1 cup fresh basil leaves, torn

1 teaspoon baby capers
4 tablespoons extra-virgin
   olive oil
3 tablespoons red wine vinegar
1 clove garlic, crushed
salt and freshly ground black
   pepper

Cut the crusts off the bread and discard. Tear the bread into small pieces, place in a medium bowl and drizzle with the water, to moisten.

Add the tomatoes, cucumbers, onion, basil and capers.

Whisk the olive oil, vinegar and garlic in a small bowl and season with salt and pepper. Pour dressing over the salad and toss to combine. Cover with food wrap and set aside for 20 minutes, to let the flavors develop.

Soft Polenta

SERVES 4

2 cups water
2¼ cups milk
4½ ounce fine polenta
  (cornmeal)
1 cup grated Parmesan cheese
3 tablespoons butter
salt

Place the water and milk in a large, heavy-based saucepan and bring to a boil. Decrease the heat to low–medium and gradually pour in the polenta, whisking continuously, until incorporated. Decrease the heat to low and cook, stirring with a wooden spoon, for 10–15 minutes, until smooth. Stir in the Parmesan cheese and butter. Season with salt.

Stuffed Roasted Tomatoes

SERVES 4

2 cups coarsely chopped
 breadcrumbs, made using
 day-old country-style bread
4 tablespoons olive oil
8 medium vine-ripened
 tomatoes
3½ ounces provolone, diced
4 tablespoons grated Pecorino
 cheese
2 tablespoons chopped pitted
 kalamata olives

4 anchovy fillets, sliced
1 clove garlic, finely chopped
2 tablespoons chopped fresh
 thyme
2 tablespoons chopped fresh
 oregano
salt and freshly ground black
 pepper

Preheat the oven to 325°F. Place the breadcrumbs on a baking pan and drizzle with half of the olive oil. Bake in the oven for 10–15 minutes, until golden. Finely chop and set aside.

Increase the oven temperature to 400°F. Slice the tops off the tomatoes and discard. Scoop out the flesh and discard.

Combine the breadcrumbs, provolone, half of the Pecorino cheese, the olives, anchovies, garlic and herbs in a medium bowl. Season with salt and pepper. Stuff the tomatoes with the filling and place on a baking sheet. Sprinkle with the remaining Pecorino cheese and drizzle with the remaining olive oil. Bake in the oven for 25–30 minutes, until tomatoes are tender but still hold their shape and stuffing is golden-brown.

Rosemary Roast Potatoes

SERVES 4

1¾ pound baby potatoes,
   washed
¼ cup olive oil
2 sprigs fresh rosemary
3 cloves garlic, sliced
salt and freshly ground black
   pepper

Preheat the oven to 400°F.

Place the potatoes in a large roasting pan. Add the olive oil, rosemary sprigs
and garlic, and toss to coat. Bake in the oven for 30–35 minutes, until tender
and golden-brown. Season with salt and pepper.

Baked Artichokes

SERVES 4

cold water, to soak artichokes
juice of 2 lemons
4 large globe artichokes, stalks
  trimmed to 1-inch
1/3 cup olive oil
3 tablespoons red-wine vinegar

2 cloves garlic, finely chopped
2 anchovy fillets, finely diced
salt and freshly ground black
  pepper
1/2 cup finely chopped fresh
  parsley

Preheat the oven to 400°F. Fill a large bowl with cold water and add the lemon juice.

Prepare the artichokes one at a time to prevent discoloration. Remove and discard the dark, tough, outer leaves, exposing the light tender ones. Trim the top third of the artichoke, creating a flat surface. Scoop out the choke, open up the outside leaves and place artichoke in the lemon water. Let soak for 10 minutes.

Combine the olive oil, vinegar, garlic and anchovies in a small bowl. Season with salt and pepper. Stir in the parsley.

Place the artichokes in a deep baking dish. Pour the olive oil mixture over the artichokes, filling up the cavities. Cover with aluminum foil and bake in the oven for 1–1½ hours, until tender.

Broad Beans with Mint & Salted Ricotta

SERVES 4

water, to blanch beans
1 pound 6 ounces young broad
  beans in their pods, shelled
2 ounces baby spinach leaves
¼ cup fresh mint leaves, torn
4 tablespoons extra-virgin
  olive oil

3 tablespoons lemon juice
salt and freshly ground black
  pepper
3 ounces salted ricotta, shaved

Bring a large pot of water to a boil. Blanch the beans for 3 minutes, until tender. Drain and rinse under cold water, to stop the cooking process. Drain again.

Combine the beans, spinach and mint in a medium bowl.

Whisk the olive oil and lemon juice together in a small bowl. Season with salt and pepper. Pour dressing over the beans and toss to coat. Serve scattered with ricotta.

Baked Fennel with Tomato & Olives

SERVES 4

butter, to prepare ovenproof
dish
salted water, to blanch fennel
bulbs
2 large fennel bulbs, trimmed
2 tablespoons olive oil
1 small onion, finely chopped
2 cloves garlic, finely chopped
¼ cup dry white wine

juice of 1 lemon
2 (14-ounce) cans diced
tomatoes
salt and freshly ground black
pepper
⅓ cup pitted kalamata olives
2 tablespoons chopped fresh
flat-leaf parsley

Preheat the oven to 350°F. Prepare an ovenproof dish with butter.

Bring a large pot of salted water to a boil. Blanch the fennel bulbs for 10–15 minutes, until tender. Drain and cut each bulb lengthwise into six pieces. Lay the pieces in a buttered ovenproof dish.

Heat the olive oil in a medium, heavy-based saucepan over low–medium heat. Add the onion and garlic, and sauté until softened. Pour in the wine and lemon juice and cook until reduced by half. Add the tomatoes, season with salt and pepper, and pour over the fennel. Scatter with olives and bake in the oven for 25–30 minutes, until fennel is tender. Sprinkle with parsley.

Marinated Grilled Zucchini

6 small zucchini, trimmed and
   sliced lengthwise into
   ¼-inch slices
2 tablespoons olive oil

MARINADE
¼ cup extra-virgin olive oil
4 tablespoons lemon juice

2 cloves garlic, finely chopped
2 tablespoons finely chopped
   fresh mint
2 tablespoons finely chopped
   fresh basil
salt and freshly ground black
   pepper

Preheat barbecue grill to high.

Lightly brush the zucchini slices with olive oil. Grill for 1 minute, turning once, until tender and golden-brown. Transfer to a medium bowl.

To make the marinade, combine the olive oil, lemon juice, garlic, mint and basil in a medium bowl. Season with salt and pepper. Pour over the zucchini, cover with food wrap and set aside in a cool place to marinate for 2 hours.

Marinated Olives

SERVES 4

9 ounces black olives
   in brine, drained
9 ounces large green olives in
   brine, drained
¾ cup extra-virgin olive oil
2 cloves garlic, finely sliced
1 tablespoon finely chopped
   fresh rosemary

1 tablespoon finely chopped
   fresh oregano
1 teaspoon finely grated lemon
   zest
½ teaspoon chili pepper flakes

Combine all the ingredients in a medium bowl. Cover and set aside to marinate
for 4 hours.

☙ Marinated olives can be stored in the refrigerator for up to 1 week. Bring them back to room
temperature before serving as the olive oil will solidify in the refrigerator.

Focaccia

SERVES 2

1 medium potato, washed
cold water, to cook potatoes
1 cup lukewarm water
1 (¼-ounce) packet dry yeast
pinch of sugar
3 cups all-purpose flour

2 tablespoons extra-virgin
   olive oil, plus extra for
   drizzling
2 tablespoons fresh rosemary
salt

Place potato in a saucepan of cold water and bring to a boil. Decrease the heat and simmer for 20–25 minutes, until tender. Drain. Peel while still warm and pass through a potato ricer or mash using a potato masher.

Combine the water, yeast and sugar together in a small bowl. Set aside in a warm place for 15 minutes to allow the yeast to develop.

Combine the potato, flour, oil and yeast mixture in a large bowl and mix until dough begins to form. Turn the dough out onto a clean counter top and knead for 10 minutes, until smooth and elastic.

Place the dough in a lightly greased bowl. Cover with a clean kitchen towel and put in a warm place in the kitchen. Let proof for 1½–2 hours, until doubled in size. Turn the dough out onto the counter top and punch out all the air.

Preheat the oven to 425°F. Heat a 10-inch metal pizza pan in the oven for 30 minutes.

Remove pan from the oven and brush with olive oil. Stretch the dough out to a large oval shape, or two smaller ones, and place on the pizza pan. Poke indentations into the dough. Cover with a kitchen towel and put in a warm place for 30 minutes, until doubled in size.

Drizzle focaccia with extra-virgin olive oil and sprinkle with rosemary and salt. Bake in the oven for 25–30 minutes, until golden-brown.

ఈ Focaccia is a flat Italian yeast bread, traditionally made with olive oil and herbs.

Caprese Salad

SERVES 4

4 large vine-ripened tomatoes,
   sliced
9 ounces bocconcini, sliced
20 fresh basil leaves
4 tablespoons extra-virgin
   olive oil
salt and freshly ground black
   pepper

Arrange alternate layers of tomato, bocconcini slices and basil decoratively on a serving plate.

Drizzle with olive oil and season with salt and pepper.

ð Bocconcini are fresh mozzarella cheese "eggs".

Green Beans with Tomato & Anchovies

SERVES 4

water, to blanch green beans
1 pound 6 ounces green beans,
  trimmed
3 tablespoons extra-virgin
  olive oil
4 anchovy fillets, finely
  chopped

3 medium vine-ripened
  tomatoes, diced
2 tablespoons lemon juice
2 tablespoons chopped frsh
  flat-leaf parsley
salt and freshly ground black
  pepper

Bring a large pot of water to a boil. Blanch the green beans for 2–3 minutes, or until just tender. Drain.

Heat the olive oil in a large fry pan. Add the anchovies and sauté until dissolved. Add the tomatoes, lemon juice and parsley, and cook until just softened. Season with salt and pepper. Add the green beans to the pan and toss to coat.

Eggplant with Tomato & Olives
Caponata

SERVES 4

2 large eggplants, cut into
  cubes
¼ cup salt
4 medium tomatoes
water, to blanch tomatoes and
  refresh
½ cup olive oil
1 red onion, diced
3 stalks celery from the center
  of the celery head, diced

2 cloves garlic, sliced
3½ ounces pitted green olives
⅓ cup red-wine vinegar
3 tablespoons baby capers,
  rinsed
1 tablespoon raisins
1 tablespoon sugar
¼ cup chopped fresh flat-leaf
  parsley
salt and ground black pepper

Place the eggplant in a colander, sprinkle with salt and toss to coat. Place the colander in a bowl and set aside to drain for 45 minutes. Rinse off the salt and pat eggplant dry with paper towels.

Bring a medium saucepan of water to a boil. Score the tomatoes, making a cross in the base of each with a sharp knife. Blanch the tomatoes in the boiling water for 10 seconds, remove using a slotted spoon and refresh in cold water. Peel off the skin and dice the flesh.

Heat half the olive oil in a large, heavy-based fry pan over medium heat. Add the eggplant and fry until soft and golden-brown. Remove using a slotted spoon and drain on paper towels.

Heat the remaining olive oil in the pan. Add the onion, celery and garlic, and sauté until golden. Decrease the heat to low, add the tomatoes and cook for 10 minutes, until softened. Add the eggplant, olives, vinegar, capers, raisins and sugar, and cook for 15–20 minutes, until sauce thickens. Stir in the parsley and season with salt and pepper.

Sweet Peppers Stewed with Tomatoes

Peperonata

SERVES 4

4 tablespoons extra-virgin
    olive oil
1 small onion, sliced
1 clove garlic, thinly sliced
3 large red bell peppers,
    thickly sliced lengthwise
3 large yellow bell peppers,
    thickly sliced lengthwise

2 medium tomatoes, diced
3 tablespoons white-wine
    vinegar
2 tablespoons finely chopped
    fresh oregano
1 teaspoon sugar
salt and freshly ground black
    pepper

Heat the olive oil in a medium, heavy-based saucepan over low–medium heat. Add the onion and garlic, and sauté until softened. Add the bell peppers and cook for 10–15 minutes, until they begin to soften. Add the tomatoes, vinegar, oregano and sugar, and cook an additional 15 minutes, until softened and flavors have developed. Season with salt and pepper.

Serve hot or cold as an accompaniment to lamb, fish or grilled steak.

❧ Bell peppers are also known as sweet peppers.

Braised Endive

SERVES 4

4 heads Belgium or French
   endive, trimmed and cored
¾ cup chicken stock
6 tablespoons butter
3½ ounces pancetta, thinly
   sliced
freshly ground black pepper
1 cup breadcrumbs, made from
   day-old country-style bread
1 cup grated Parmesan cheese

Preheat the oven to 350°F.

Cut the endive in half lengthwise and place in an ovenproof dish. Pour in the chicken stock and dot with butter. Sprinkle with pancetta and season with pepper.

Cover with aluminum foil and bake in the oven for 15–20 minutes, until tender. Remove the foil and sprinkle with breadcrumbs and Parmesan cheese. Return to the oven and bake, uncovered, an additional 10 minutes, until golden-brown.

Hot Anchovy Dipping Sauce
Bagna cauda

MAKES 1 CUP

¾ cup extra-virgin olive oil
4 cloves garlic, finely chopped
10 anchovy fillets, finely
    chopped
5 tablespoons butter

Place ¼ cup of the olive oil and the garlic in a food processor or blender and blend to form a paste.

Heat the remaining olive oil in a medium fry pan over low heat. Add the garlic paste and anchovies, and sauté until garlic has softened and anchovies have dissolved. Add the butter and stir until melted.

Serve warm, with raw or lightly steamed vegetables for dipping.

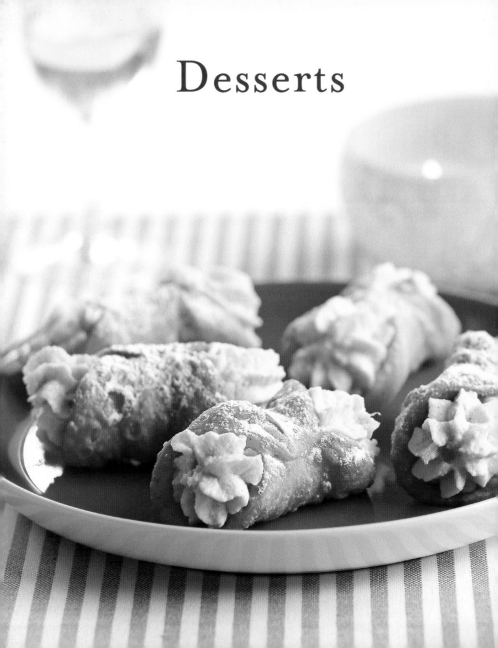

Desserts

The final course is the *dolce* or dessert. Pastries, tarts, gelato, granita, cannoli, biscotti and tiramisu are all popular. These sweets may also be eaten as a mid-morning or an afternoon pick-me-up. Flavored with candied fruits, chocolate, nuts, citrus, liqueurs and wine, they can be seen filling shop windows all over Italy.

Long Italian meals are often finished with fresh fruit and cheese, followed perhaps by an espresso and biscotti. However, on festive occasions you can be sure to find an indulgent delight or two.

‹ CANNOLI (PAGE 214)

Cannoli

vegetable oil for deep-frying
piece of bread, to test oil

DOUGH
1½ cups all-purpose flour
1½ tablespoons superfine
   (bar) sugar
½ teaspoon ground cinnamon
2 tablespoons butter, melted
⅓ cup Marsala wine
1 large egg, separated

FILLING
1¾ pounds fresh ricotta
½ cup confectioner's
   (powdered) sugar
1 teaspoon ground cinnamon
½ cup mixed candied citrus
   peel, finely chopped
¼ cup Marsala wine

To make the dough, combine the flour, superfine sugar and cinnamon in a medium bowl. Add the butter, Marsala wine and egg yolk, and stir until dough begins to form. Turn out onto a clean counter top and knead for 10 minutes, until smooth and elastic. Cover with food wrap and refrigerate for 30 minutes.

Divide the dough into quarters. Lightly flour the counter top and shape one piece into a small rectangle. Keep the remaining pieces covered with food wrap, to prevent drying out. Feed the dough through the thickest setting of a pasta machine a few times. Gradually work down the settings, dusting the dough occasionally with flour, until it passes through the second thinnest setting. Cut the sheet in half as it gets longer, to make it more manageable.

Cut out rounds, using an 3-inch round pastry cutter. Place the rounds on a lightly floured tray and cover with a clean kitchen towel. Roll out and cut the remaining dough.

Half-fill a large, heavy-based saucepan with vegetable oil. Heat the vegetable oil to 350°F or until a piece of bread browns in 15 seconds when tested.

Wrap a dough round around a lightly oiled cannoli tube. Moisten the overlapping edges with egg white to seal. Fry the cannoli, two at a time, for 2–3 minutes, turning until crisp and golden-brown. Remove using a slotted spoon and drain on paper towels. Slide shells off the tubes while still warm. Repeat the process with the remaining dough. Set shells aside to cool completely.

To make the filling, place the ricotta in a medium bowl. Sift in the confectioner's sugar and cinnamon. Stir in the candied citrus peel and Marsala wine until smooth. Spoon the filling into a pastry bag fitted with a large star-shaped nozzle. Fill the cooled shells and dust with confectioner's sugar.

❧ Cannoli shells can be purchased from specialty kitchenware stores. Unfilled cannoli shells can be stored in an airtight container for up to 1 month.

Chocolate Bread & Butter Pudding
Budino nero

SERVES 6

1 cup cream
1 cup milk
4½ ounces dark chocolate,
   coarsely chopped
4 large egg yolks
⅓ cup superfine (bar) sugar

½ teaspoon vanilla extract
5 ounces panettone (rich
   fruited Italian yeast bread),
   sliced
hot water, to fill baking dish

Preheat the oven to 350°F. Lightly grease six 6-fluid ounce ramekins with butter.

Place the cream and milk in a medium saucepan over medium heat and bring almost to boiling point. Remove from heat, add the chocolate and stir until smooth. Set aside.

Whisk the egg yolks, superfine sugar and vanilla together, until pale and thick. Gradually pour in the hot chocolate mixture, stirring to combine. Arrange panettone slices in prepared ramekins. Pour chocolate mixture over the tops, pressing down so the bread is soaked.

Place the ramekins in a baking dish. Pour enough hot water into the dish to come half way up the sides of the ramekins. Bake in the oven for 25–30 minutes, until firm. Remove from the oven and let puddings cool for 20 minutes. Carefully remove ramekins from the dish. Serve warm with cream.

Zuppa Inglese

SERVES 6–8

10½ ounces store-bought
plain sponge cake, cut into
³/8-inch thick slices
⅓ cup rum
1 cup thickened cream
fresh raspberries, to decorate
½ cup sliced almonds, lightly
toasted (optional)

CUSTARD
2 cups milk
1 vanilla bean, split lengthwise
and seeds scraped

5 large egg yolks
½ cup superfine (bar) sugar
3 tablespoons all-purpose
flour

RASPBERRY SAUCE
1 pound 2 ounces fresh or
frozen raspberries
¼ cup sugar
2 tablespoons rum

To make the custard, heat the milk and vanilla bean and seeds in a medium saucepan over low–medium heat, until it almost reaches the boiling point. Remove from heat.

Using an electric mixer, beat the egg yolks and superfine sugar together until pale and creamy. Stir in the flour. Discard the vanilla bean and gradually pour the hot milk into the yolk mixture, stirring to combine. Return mixture to the pan and cook over low heat, stirring until thickened. Do not boil. >

Remove from heat and transfer to a bowl. Cover with a piece of parchment (baking) paper to prevent a skin from forming and refrigerate until cooled.

To make the raspberry sauce, place the raspberries, sugar and rum in a medium saucepan over low–medium heat. Cook for 10 minutes, until thickened. Transfer to a food processor or blender and blend until puréed. Pass through a fine mesh sieve.

To assemble the trifle, line the bottom of a 1½ quart capacity glass bowl with a third of the sponge cake slices. Sprinkle with a third of the rum. Spoon over a third of the custard followed by half the raspberry purée. Repeat the layers twice more, finishing with the custard. Cover with food wrap and refrigerate for at least 3 hours, to allow the flavors to develop.

Whip the cream in a medium bowl using an electric mixer, until soft peaks form. Spread the cream over the trifle and decorate with fresh raspberries and toasted almonds, if desired.

๛ Zuppa Inglese (Italian for "English Soup") is a custard-based dessert related to English truffle.

Espresso Granita

SERVES 4

¼ cup superfine (bar) caster
   sugar
¼ cup water
2 cups espresso coffee

Place the sugar and water in a small saucepan and bring to a boil. Decrease the heat to low and gently simmer, stirring occasionally, until the sugar has dissolved. Pour in the espresso and stir to combine.

Pour into a shallow container and set aside to cool slightly. Freeze for 20 minutes, or until partially set. Stir with a fork to break up the ice crystals. Return to the freezer and repeat the process again.

Spoon into serving glasses and top with whipped cream.

ᐬ Granita is an Italian semi-frozen dessert related to sorbet and Italian ice.

Orange Ricotta Fritters

MAKES 24

1 pound 2 ounces fresh ricotta
  cheese
3 large eggs, lightly beaten
2 tablespoons dark rum
1 tablespoon finely grated
  orange zest
½ cup all-purpose flour

1 teaspoon baking powder
vegetable oil, for deep-frying
piece of bread, to test oil
6 tablespoons honey
confectioner's (powdered)
  sugar, for dusting

Beat the ricotta, eggs, rum and orange zest together in a medium bowl. Sift in the flour and baking powder and stir to combine.

Half fill a large, heavy-based saucepan with vegetable oil. Heat the vegetable oil to 350°F or until a piece of bread browns in 15 seconds when tested. Carefully drop tablespoons of ricotta mixture into the vegetable oil and fry in batches, turning until puffed and golden-brown. Remove using a slotted spoon and drain on paper towels.

Serve immediately, drizzled with honey and dusted with confectioner's sugar.

Pine Nut Tart

SERVES 6–8

PASTRY

5 ounces softened unsalted
butter, cubed

½ cup confectioner's
(powdered) sugar

2 large egg yolks

1²/₃ cups all-purpose flour

1½ tablespoons ice water

FILLING

6 tablespoons honey

1 tablespoon lemon juice

4 ouces softened butter

½ cup firmly packed soft
brown sugar

1 teaspoon finely grated lemon
zest

½ teaspoon vanilla extract

3 large eggs

1½ cups pine nuts, lightly
toasted

To make the pastry, beat butter and sugar together using an electric mixer, until pale and creamy. Beat in the eggs, one at a time, until combined. Mix in the flour and enough ice water to bring the dough together. Remove from the bowl, shape into a ball, cover with food wrap and refrigerate for 30 minutes.

Preheat the oven to 350°F. Lightly grease a 9-inch tart pan with removable bottom. >

Roll out the pastry onto a lightly floured counter top to ⅛-inch thick. Press into tart pan and refrigerate for 30 minutes.

Remove the tart pan from the refrigerator, cover with parchment (baking) paper and fill with pastry weights or raw rice. Bake in the oven for 20 minutes, until light golden. Set aside to cool.

To make the filling, heat the honey and lemon juice together in a small saucepan over low heat, until a thin sauce forms. Set aside to cool. Cream the butter, sugar, lemon zest and vanilla using an electric mixer, until pale and creamy. Add the eggs, one at a time, mixing to combine. Add the honey mixture and pine nuts, and stir to combine. Spoon into the prepared tart pan. Bake for 40 minutes, until set and golden-brown.

Baked Peaches with Zabaglione

SERVES 4

PEACHES
4 ripe peaches, halved and
    pitted
¼ cup sweet white wine
3 tablespoons butter

ZABAGLIONE
4 large egg yolks
¼ cup superfine (bar) sugar
⅓ cup Marsala wine
barely simmering water, to
    cook zabaglione

Preheat the oven to 350°F.

Place the peaches, cut side up, in an ovenproof dish. Drizzle with Marsala wine and dot with butter. Bake in the oven for 20–30 minutes, until golden-brown.

To make the zabaglione, whisk the egg yolks and sugar together in a medium heatproof bowl, until thick and creamy. Add the Marsala wine. Place bowl over a saucepan of barely simmering water and cook, whisking continuously, until mixture has tripled in volume. Do not allow the bowl to get too hot as this will cause the eggs to scramble.

Arrange the baked peaches on serving plates or in bowls and spoon the zabaglione over.

&ifmmp; Zabaglione is an Italian custard, also known as zabayon or sabayon.

Chocolate, Ricotta & Hazelnut Ravioli

MAKES 12

DOUGH

¾ cup all-purpose flour, plus
  more for dusting
1 tablespoon superfine (bar)
  sugar
½ teaspoon ground cinnamon
1 tablespoon butter, melted
2 tablespoons Marsala wine
1 large egg, separated

FILLING

5 ounces fresh ricotta, drained
4 tablespoons confectioner's
  (powdered) sugar, plus
  more for dusting
½ teaspoon ground cinnamon
4 tablespoons ground
  hazelnuts
2 teaspoons cocoa
vegetable oil for frying
piece of bread, to test vegetable
  oil

To make the dough, combine the flour, sugar and cinnamon together in a medium bowl. Add the butter, Marsala wine and egg yolk, and stir until dough begins to form. Turn dough out onto a clean counter top and knead for 10 minutes, until it becomes smooth and elastic. Cover with food wrap and refrigerate for 30 minutes.

To make the filling, place the ricotta in a small bowl. Sift in the confectioner's sugar, cocoa and cinnamon. Add the hazelnuts and stir to combine. >

Divide the dough in half. Lightly flour a counter top and shape one portion into a small rectangle. Keep the remaining piece covered in food wrap, to prevent drying. Feed the dough through the thickest setting of a pasta machine a few times. Gradually work down the settings, dusting the dough occasionally with flour, until it passes through the second thinnest setting. Cut the sheet in half as it gets longer, to make it more manageable.

Trim each dough sheet into two even lengths. Place six evenly spaced spoonfuls of filling along one of the sheets and brush the edges of the dough with egg white. Lay the second sheet of dough over the top and press around the filling to seal and remove any trapped air. Cut the ravioli into squares using a fluted pasta cutter or sharp knife, and place onto a lightly floured tray.

Repeat the process with the remaining dough and filling.

Half-fill a large, heavy-based saucepan with vegetable oil. Heat the vegetable oil to 350°F or until a piece of bread browns in 15 seconds when tested. Fry the ravioli in batches, for 2–3 minutes, turning, until crisp and golden-brown. Remove using a slotted spoon and drain on paper towel.

Dust with confectioner's sugar and serve immediately.

Tiramisu

SERVES 8

4 large eggs, separated
½ cup superfine (bar) sugar
1 pound 2 ounces mascarpone
⅓ cup brandy

¾ cup espresso coffee
20 savoiardi (Italian sponge
    finger biscuits)
dutch cocoa, for dusting

Beat the egg yolks and sugar together in a medium bowl until thick and pale. Add the mascarpone and 2 tablespoons of the brandy and stir to combine.

Using an electric mixer, whip the egg whites until soft peaks form. Stir one third of the egg whites into the mascarpone mixture, then gently fold in the remainder.

Combine the coffee and remaining brandy in a small bowl. Dip half the biscuits, one at a time, in the coffee mixture to moisten. Arrange in a single layer in a deep 8-inch square dish. Spread with half the mascarpone mixture and dust with cocoa. Repeat layers. Cover with food wrap and refrigerate for at least 4 hours.

To serve, dust generously with cocoa.

Amaretti Baked Apples

SERVES 4

4 tart cooking apples, such as
    Granny Smith
crème fraîche or mascarpone,
    to serve (optional)

SYRUP
1½ cups apple juice
2 tablespoons honey

FILLING
4 amaretti biscuits, crushed
2 tablespoons ground walnuts
2 tablespoons ground almonds
1 tablespoon soft brown sugar
1 tablespoon softened butter
1 teaspoon lemon zest
½ teaspoon ground cinnamon

Preheat the oven to 350°F.

Heat the apple juice and honey together in a small saucepan over low heat, until the honey melts. Set aside.

To make the filling, combine the amaretti biscuits, ground walnuts and almonds, sugar, butter, lemon zest and cinnamon together in a small bowl.

Core the apples and score the skin around the circumference, so that they split neatly during cooking. Stuff the apples with amaretti filling and arrange upright in a small baking dish. Pour the syrup around the apples and bake, uncovered, for 35–45 minutes, until tender. Serve drizzled with syrup, with crème fraîche or mascarpone if desired.

☙ Amaretti are Italian almond-flavored macaroons.

Vanilla Panna Cotta

SERVES 4

sweet almond oil or unflavored
   oil, to prepare ramekins
2 cups heavy cream
½ cup superfine (bar) sugar
2 vanilla beans, split
   lengthwise and seeds
   scraped

2 gelatin leaves
cold water, to soften gelatin
   leaves
berries, to serve

Lightly prepare four 4-fluid ounce capacity ramekins with sweet almond or unflavored oil.

Combine the cream, sugar and vanilla beans and seeds in a medium saucepan and bring almost to boiling point. Decrease the heat and gently simmer for 5 minutes.

Soak the gelatin leaves in a small bowl of cold water, until softened. Squeeze out the water and stir leaves into the cream mixture. Strain cream through a fine mesh sieve into a pitcher. Set aside to cool slightly.

Pour the cream into the prepared ramekins and refrigerate for 6 hours, or until set. To turn out, run a small knife around the edge of each panna cotta to loosen, and invert onto a serving plate.

Serve with seasonal berries.

⌒ In gereral, two gelatin leaves are equal to one teaspoon of powdered gelatin.

Walnut Tart
Torta di noci

vegetable oil, to prepare pan
1 egg yolk, for glazing
confectioner's (powdered)
   sugar, for dusting

PASTRY
8 ounces softened butter
3 cups all-purpose flour
1 cup superfine (bar) sugar
1 teaspoon ground cinnamon
3 large egg yolks
2 teaspoons lemon zest

FILLING
7 ounces walnut halves
3 ($^3/_8$-inch) thick slices
   sourdough bread, crusts
   removed and coarsely
   chopped
6 tablespoons honey
2 tablespoons dark rum

To make the pastry, rub the butter into the flour in a medium bowl, until mixture resembles coarse breadcrumbs. Stir in the superfine sugar and cinnamon. Add the egg yolks and zest, and mix until dough begins to form. Shape the dough into a round, cover with food wrap and refrigerate for 30 minutes.

Preheat the oven to 375°F. Lightly prepare an 8-inch tart pan that has a removable bottom with vegetable oil.

To make the filling, place the walnuts and bread into a food processor or blender and pulse to make coarse crumbs. Transfer to a medium bowl.

Heat the honey and rum in a small saucepan until thin sauce forms. Pour over the walnut mixture and stir to combine. Set aside to cool.

Divide the pastry into two pieces. Roll out one portion between two pieces of lightly greased parchment (baking) paper and fit into the prepared pan, leaving the edges hanging over a little. Sprinkle the filling over the top of the pastry.

Roll out the remaining piece of pastry in the same way and lay it over the filling. Pinch the edges together to seal, and trim off any excess pastry. Make a few holes in the top, for steam to escape, and brush with egg yolk.

Bake in the oven for 30–35 minutes, until golden-brown. Allow to cool in the pan for 10 minutes. Remove tart from the pan and place on a wire rack to cool completely. Dust heavily with confectioner's sugar.

☞ Torta di noci is Italin flourless walnut cake.

Limoncello & Mascarpone Gelato

SERVES 4–6

½ cup freshly squeezed lemon
  juice
½ cup milk
6 large egg yolks
1 cup superfine (bar) sugar

1 teaspoon lemon zest
½ cup limoncello (Italian
  lemon) liqueur
1 pound 2 ounces mascarpone

Place the lemon juice in a small saucepan over medium–high heat and simmer until reduced by half. Set aside to cool.

Heat the milk in a medium saucepan over low–medium heat, until it almost reaches boiling point. Remove from the heat.

Beat the egg yolks, sugar and lemon zest together in a medium bowl, until pale and thick. Gradually pour the hot milk into the yolk mixture, stirring to combine. Return mixture to the pan and cook over low heat, stirring, until slightly thickened. Do not boil. Remove from the heat, transfer to a bowl and refrigerate until cooled.

Add the reduced lemon juice and limoncello to the yolk mixture. Stir through the mascarpone. Pour into an ice-cream machine and churn, according to manufacturer's instructions, until frozen. Transfer to a freezer proof container and freeze for 3 hours, or until ready to serve.

Torrone Semifreddo

SERVES 12

almond oil, to prepare pan
½ cup milk
6 large egg yolks
1 cup superfine (bar) sugar
1 teaspoon vanilla extract

1 tablespoon lemon juice
1 teaspoon lemon zest
3 cups cream
7 ounces torrone (Italian
　　nougat candy), chopped

Line a 4-inch × 8½-inch loaf pan with aluminum foil, followed by a double layer of food wrap (leaving a 4-inch overhang on both sides). Lightly cover with almond oil.

Place the milk in a small saucepan over medium heat and bring to a boil.

Beat the egg yolks, sugar and vanilla until pale and thick. Gradually pour in the hot milk and beat for 5–8 minutes, until cooled. Stir in the lemon juice and zest. Cover with food wrap and refrigerate until chilled.

In a separate bowl whip the cream until soft peaks form. Fold cream and torrone into the chilled egg mixture. Pour into prepared pan and fold food wrap over to cover. Freeze for 4–6 hours, until frozen but not too hard.

ॐ Semifreddo (italian for "half cold") is a chilled or partially frozen dessert. Torrone can be purchased from Italian grocers. Substitute with conventional nougat if unable to find.

Orange & Fig Ricotta Cake

SERVES 10–12

almond oil, to prepare cake
  pan
zest and juice of 2 oranges
1½ cups finely chopped dried
  figs
1 pound 6 ounces firm ricotta

3 whole large eggs, plus 9 large
  eggs, separated
¾ cup candied citrus peel
1 cup superfine (bar) sugar
1 cup all-purpose flour
½ cup sliced almonds

Preheat the oven to 350°F. Lightly prepare a 10-inch round springform cake pan with almond oil and line the bottom with parchment (baking) paper.

Heat the orange juice and zest in a small saucepan over low–medium heat. Add the figs and set aside to soak for 20 minutes.

Whisk the ricotta, whole eggs, egg yolks, candied citrus peel, sugar and flour in a large bowl, until combined. Stir in the soaked figs and juice mixture.

Whisk the egg whites in a medium bowl until stiff peaks form. Fold one third of the whites through the fig mixture and then fold through the remainder. Pour into the prepared pan and sprinkle with sliced almonds. Bake in the oven for 60 minutes, until the center is firm to touch and a skewer comes out clean when tested. Let the cake to cool in the pan for 10 minutes before turning out onto a rack to cool completely.

Pistachio & Almond Biscotti

MAKES ABOUT 50 BISCOTTI

¾ cup superfine (bar) sugar

2 large eggs

1 teaspoon vanilla extract

1 teaspoon orange zest

2 cups all-purpose flour, plus
more for shaping dough

1 teaspoon baking powder

¹/₃ cup pistachios

¹/₃ cup whole almonds

Preheat the oven to 350°F. Line two baking sheets with parchment (baking) paper.

Beat the sugar, eggs, vanilla and orange zest together, until thick and pale. Sift in the flour and baking powder. Add the pistachios and almonds, and stir to combine. Turn the mixture out onto a lightly floured counter top. Divide the dough in half and shape into logs approximately 10-inches long.

Place logs onto the prepared baking sheets and flatten slightly. Bake in the oven for 20–25 minutes, until firm. Remove from the oven and set aside to cool.

Decrease oven temperature to 275°. Cut the logs into thick slices. Place on baking sheets and bake in the oven for 15 minutes, until golden and crisp. Transfer onto a wire rack to cool completely.

☞ Biscotti are crisp Italian twice-baked cookies. Store biscotti in an airtight container for up to 1 month.

Special Ingredients

AGNOLOTTI Semi-circular pockets of pasta stuffed with a mix of cheese and meats, or puréed vegetables. The name means 'lamb's ears'.

ARANCINI Cold risotto rolled in bread crumbs and fried until golden-brown and warmed through.

ARBORIO A short-grain rice used to make risotto. Other varieties used for risotto are carnaroli and vialone.

BRESAOLA Air-dried salted beef. Substitute with prosciutto if unable to find.

BUCATINI Thick spaghetti-shaped tubular pasta.

CANNELLONI Large tubes of pasta, suitable for stuffing.

CAVOLO NERO A long-leafed variety of winter cabbage. Substitute with cabbage or curly kale if unable to find.

CORNICHONS Little pickled cucumbers.

CRÈME FRAÎCHE A type of soured cream that is thicker and milder in flavor than regular sour cream.

CROSTINI Thin slices of bread, usually cut from a baguette, that are either lightly browned under the grill or fried in butter or oil.

FARFALLE Pasta resembling bow ties or butterflies.

FETTUCINE Long flat ribbons of pasta.

FONTINA CHEESE An Italian cheese made from cow's milk, suitable for melting.

FUSILLI Pasta spirals.

GNOCCHI Small dumplings made from a dough of mashed potato or flour.

GORGONZOLA A creamy blue cheese made from cow's milk.

GRANA PADANO A mild Parmesan cheese that has been aged for six months; *see also* Parmigiano-Reggiano.

LIMONCELLO An Italian spirit infused with lemon zest.

MASCARPONE A thick creamy cheese made from fresh cream.

ORECCHIETTE Pasta shaped like small bowls—the name means 'little ears' in Italian.

PANCETTA A dry-cured meat that has been salted and spiced. Made from the pork belly, it can be 'rolled' or 'flat'.

PANETTONE Italian yeast cake made with dried fruit and candied peel.

PAPPARDELLE Long flat wide ribbons of pasta.

PARMESAN Sharp-flavored cheese made from cow's milk; *see also* Parmigiano-Reggiano.

PARMIGIANO-REGGIANO A hard, sharp-flavored cheese made from cow's milk and aged for at least fourteen months. The white matrix insignia covering the rind is what separates it from other grana or Parmesans. Well-known varieties are *grana padano* (a milder cheese aged for six months that is particularly good for grating) and *pecorino* (sold fresh or aged, also good for grating).

PASSATA A sauce made from fresh tomatoes that have been put through a food mill.

PECORINO A variety of Parmesan cheese. *See also* Parmigiano-Reggiano.

POLENTA Flavored with stock or butter during the cooking stage, polenta (also known as cornmeal) can be soft, baked or grilled, and is usually served as a side dish.

PROSCIUTTO An Italian ham that has been salted and then air-dried for up to two years.

PROVOLONE A semi-hard Italian cheese. There are numerous varieties, with flavors ranging from sharp and strong to sweet and mild.

RISONI Small, grain-shaped pasta, similar in appearance to grains of rice.

SQUID INK The black ink of the squid, it is mild in flavor and can be used to color pasta or rice.

WITLOF Related to the endive, this leafy green has a slightly bitter taste.

Index

PENGUIN BOOKS

Published by the Penguin Group
Penguin Group (USA) Inc., 375 Hudson Street, New York, New York 10014, USA
Penguin Group (Canada), 90 Eglinton Avenue East, Suite 700, Toronto, Ontario M4P 2Y3, Canada
(a division of Pearson Penguin Canada Inc.)
Penguin Books Ltd, 80 Strand, London WC2R 0RL, England
Penguin Ireland, 25 St Stephen's Green, Dublin 2, Ireland (a division of Penguin Books Ltd)
Penguin Group (Australia), 707 Collins Street, Melbourne, Victoria 3008, Australia
(a division of Pearson Australia Group Pty Ltd)
Penguin Books India Pvt Ltd, 11 Community Centre, Panchsheel Park, New Delhi–110 017, India
Penguin Group (NZ), 67 Apollo Drive, Rosedale, Auckland 0632, New Zealand (a division of Pearson New Zealand Ltd)
Penguin Books (South Africa), Rosebank Office Park, 181 Jan Smuts Avenue, Parktown North 2193, South Africa
Penguin China, B7 Jiaming Center, 27 East Third Ring Road North, Chaoyang District, Beijing 100020, China

PENGUIN BOOKS LTD, REGISTERED OFFICES: 80 STRAND, LONDON WC2R 0RL, ENGLAND

Previously published in Australia as *Italian Bible* under ISBN: 978-0-14-320287-5

This edition published in 2012 by Penguin Group (USA) Inc.
Special Markets ISBN 978-0-14-219663-2

10 9 8 7 6 5 4 3 2

Text and photographs copyright © Penguin Group (Australia), 2010

The moral right of the author has been asserted

Designed by Claire Tice and Marley Flory © Penguin Group (Australia)
Photography by Julie Renouf
Food styling by Lee Blaylock
Typeset by Post Pre-press Group, Brisbane, Queensland
Scans and separations by Splitting Image, P/L, Clayton, Victoria

Printed in the United States of America

ALWAYS LEARNING   **PEARSON**